The Internet Con

T0182529

The Internet Con

How to Seize the Means of Computation

Cory Doctorow

VERSO

London • New York

This paperback edition first published by Verso 2024
First published by Verso 2023
© Cory Doctorow 2023

The moral rights of the author have been asserted

1 3 5 7 9 10 8 6 4 2

Verso
UK: 6 Meard Street, London W1F 0EG
US: 388 Atlantic Avenue, Brooklyn, NY 11217
versobooks.com

Verso is the imprint of New Left Books

ISBN-13: 978-1-80429-214-3

British Library Cataloguing in Publication Data
A catalogue record for this book is available from the British Library

Library of Congress Cataloging-in-Publication Data
A catalog record for this book is available from the Library of Congress

Typeset in Sabon by MJ & N Gavan, Truro, Cornwall
Printed and bound by CPI Group (UK) Ltd, Croydon, CRO 4YY

For Ada Lovelace and Alan Turing,
for giving us universal computers.

Contents

Introduction

This is a book for people who want to destroy Big Tech.

It's not a book for people who want to tame Big Tech. There's no fixing Big Tech.

It's not a book for people who want to get rid of technology itself. Technology isn't the problem. Stop thinking about what technology *does* and start thinking about who technology does it *to* and who it does it *for*.

This is a book about the thing Big Tech fears the most: technology operated by and for the people who use it.

Today's tech barons aren't evil geniuses.

They're not "evil"—their ambitions to world domination are neither novel nor especially grandiose. The founders of the fallen tech giants of yesteryear—Altavista and DEC and Sun Microsystems and Commodore—all wanted the same thing. The difference is, they didn't get it.

They're also not geniuses. The reason the tech industry spent generations churning as new companies and systems supplanted the old was that in the olden days, we enforced competition rules that ensured this would happen. We used to ban companies from buying their competitors and from creating vertical monopolies.

The new crop of leaders aren't being displaced, but it's not due to their incredible leadership and vision.

Forty years ago, we shot antitrust law in the guts, and we let companies led by mediocre idiots no better than their forebears establish monopolies. These donkeys were able to parlay their monopoly winnings into policies that prevented new technologies from supplanting their own. They got to decide who was allowed to compete with them, and how.

Notably, tech giants today are able to wield the law against interoperators: new technologies that plug into their services, systems and platforms. That's a privilege that none of yesterday's easily toppled tech giants had—if IBM wanted to prevent its competitors (the "seven dwarves" of the mainframe era) from making software, printers, keyboards and storage for its mainframes, it had to figure out how to build a computer that no one else could reverse engineer and improve on.

For complex reasons, this is impossible. The very bedrock of computer science—ideas named for midcentury computing demigods, like "Turing completeness" and "von Neumann machines"—dictates that the creation of noninteroperable computers is a fool's errand. It's fantasy, not science fiction, like a time machine or a faster-than-light drive.

Today's tech giants have not invented an interop-proof computer. They've invented laws that make interoperability illegal unless they give permission for it. A new, complex thicket of copyright, patent, trade secret, noncompete and other IP rights has conjured up a new offense we can think of as "felony contempt of business model"—the right of large firms to dictate how their customers, competitors and even their critics must use their products.

Why do they fear interop so much? Simple: switching costs.

Whenever economists gather to handwave away the rise of Big Tech as a historical inevitability, they will make frequent reference to "network effects." This is a term of art for products that get more valuable every time they win a new customer: you join Facebook to chat with the people who are already there, and then new users join Facebook because *you* are there.

But network effects are merely how Big Tech gets big. *Switching costs* are how Big Tech *stays* big.

Switching costs are all the things you have to give up when you *stop* using a product or service. Quit Facebook and you lose the family photos you've uploaded and access to the friends, family, community and customers you go there to hang out with.

When switching costs are high enough, people will keep using products and services even though they hate those products and services. So long as the pain of staying is less than the pain of leaving, users stay. That means that if companies can raise their switching costs, they can also treat their customers worse—and still keep their business.

The corollary: the *lower* the switching costs are, the *better* a company has to treat you if they want to keep your business. If users who quit Facebook—resigned their accounts, deleted the app—could *still talk to their Facebook friends* through a rival service that could interchange messages with it, then Facebook would be in serious trouble.

Interoperability lowers switching costs. Interoperability allows us, the users of technology, to set the terms on which we use that technology. It allows us to use the parts of products and services that benefit us, and block the parts that don't.

There are a lot of things we should do to fix Big Tech: change the rules for mergers, pass comprehensive privacy legislation, ban deceptive "dark patterns" and break up big companies into smaller, competing firms

These will take a long time.

How long? It took *sixty-nine years* for the US government to break up AT&T.

By contrast, interop is immediate. Make it legal for new technologies to plug into existing ones—that is, make it legal to blast holes in every walled garden—and users (that's us) get immediate, profound relief: relief from manipulation, high-handed moderation, surveillance, price-gouging, disgusting or misleading algorithmic suggestions ... the whole panoply of technology's sins.

This is a book that explains:

- What interoperability is
- How interoperability works
- How we can get interoperability
- How we can mitigate interoperability's problems

It explains the different kinds of interoperability, from widely adopted formal standards to the guerrilla warfare of reverse engineering. It unpacks the legislative and judicial history of the war on interoperability. It sets out a diversity of tactics—commercial, legal, technological and social—to foster interoperability. It explains how well-constructed interoperability policy is sturdy enough to beat the attacks against it, be they legal, technical, social or commercial.

This is a shovel-ready book. It explains, in nontechnical language, how to dismantle Big Tech's control over our digital lives and devolve control to the people who suffer most under Big Tech's hegemony: marginalized users, low-level tech workers and the people who live downstream of tech's exhaust plume: people choking on toxic waste from the tech industry and people living under dictatorships where control is maintained with off-the-shelf cyberweapons used to hunt opposition figures.

PART I

Seize the Means of Computation

1

How Big Tech Got Big

"Tech exceptionalism" is the sin of thinking that the normal rules don't apply to technology.

The idea that you can lose money on every transaction but make it up with scale (looking at you, Uber)? Pure tech exceptionalism.

The idea that you can take an unjust system like racist policing practices and fix it with technology? Exceptionalism. The idea that tech itself *can't* be racist because computers are just doing math, and math can't be racist? Utter exceptionalism.

Tech critics are usually good at pointing out tech exceptionalism when they see it, but there's one tech exceptionalist blind spot. There's one place where tech boosters and critics come together to sing the same song.

Both tech's biggest boosters and its most savage critics agree that tech leaders—the Zuckerbergs, Jobses, Bezoses, Musks, Gateses, Brins and Pages—are brilliant. Now, the boosters will tell you that these men are *good* geniuses whose singular vision and leadership have transformed the world; while the critics will tell you that these are *evil* geniuses whose singular vision and leadership have transformed the world … for the worse.

But one thing they all agree on: these guys are geniuses.

I get it. The empires our tech bro overlords built are some of the most valuable, influential companies in human history. They have bigger budgets than many nations. Their users outnumber the populations of any nation on Earth.

What's more, it wasn't always thus. Prior to the mid-2000s, tech was a dynamic, chaotic roil of new startups that rose to prominence and became household names in a few short years, only to be vanquished just as they were peaking, when a new company entered the market and toppled them.

Somehow, these new giants—the companies that have, in the words of New Zealand software developer Tom Eastman, transformed the internet into "a group of five websites, each consisting of screenshots of text from the other four"—interrupted that cycle of "disruption." They didn't just *get* big, they *stayed* big, and then they got bigger.

How did these tech companies succeed in maintaining the dominance that so many of their predecessors failed to attain? Was it their vision? Was it their leadership?

Nope.

If tech were led by exceptional geniuses whose singular vision made it impossible to unseat them, then you'd expect that the structure of the tech industry itself would be exceptional. That is, you'd expect that tech's mass-extinction event, which turned the wild and wooly web into a few giant websites, was unique to tech, driven by those storied geniuses.

But that's not the case at all. Nearly every industry in the world looks like the tech industry: dominated by a handful of giant companies that emerged out of a cataclysmic, forty-year die-off of smaller firms which either failed or were folded into the surviving giants.

Here's a partial list of concentrated industries from the Open Markets Institute—industries where between one and five companies account for the vast majority of business: pharmaceuticals, health insurers, appliances, athletic shoes, defense contractors, book publishing, booze, drug stores, office supplies, eyeglasses, LCD glass, glass bottles, vitamin C, car parts, bottle caps, airlines, railroads, mattresses, Lasik lasers, cowboy boots and candy.

If tech's consolidation is down to the exceptional genius of its leaders, then they are part of a bumper crop of exceptional geniuses who all managed to rise to prominence in their respective firms and then steer them into positions where they crushed, bought or sidelined all their competitors over the past forty years or so.

Occam's Razor posits that the simplest explanation is most likely to be true. For that reason, I think we can safely reject the idea that sunspots, water contaminants or gamma rays caused an exceptional generation of business leaders to be conceived all at the same time, all over the world.

Likewise, I am going to discount the possibility that, in the 1970s and 1980s, aliens came to Earth and knocked up the future mothers of a new subrace of elite CEOs whose extraterrestrial DNA conferred upon them the power to steer companies to total industrial dominance.

Not only do those explanations stretch the imagination, but they also ignore a simpler, far more tangible explanation for the incredible die-off of businesses in every industry. Forty years ago, countries all over the world altered the basis on which they enforced their competition laws—often called "antitrust" laws— to be more tolerant of monopolies. Forty years later, we have a lot of monopolies.

These facts are related.

Let's have a quick refresher course on antitrust law, shall we? Antitrust was born in the late nineteenth century, when American industries had been consolidated through "trusts." A trust is an organization that holds something of value "in trust" for someone else. For example, you might live near a conservation area that a group of donors bought and handed over to a trust to preserve and maintain. The trust is run by "trustees"—directors who oversee its assets.

In the nineteenth century, American robber barons got together and formed trusts: for example, a group of railroad owners could sell their shares to a "railroad trust" and become beneficiaries of the trust. The trustees—the same robber barons, or their representatives—would run the trust, deciding how to operate all these different, nominally competing railroads to maximize the return to the trustees (the railroads' former owners).

A trust was a way of merging all the dominant companies in a single industry (or even multiple related industries, like oil refineries, railroads, pipelines and oil wells) into a single company, while maintaining the fiction that all of these companies were their own businesses.

Any company that *didn't* sell to the trust was quickly driven to its knees. For example, if you owned a freight company and wouldn't sell out to the trust, all the railroads you depended on to carry your freight would charge you more than they'd charge your competitors for carrying the same freight—or they'd refuse to carry your freight at all.

What's more, any business that supplied a trust would quickly find itself stripped of its profit margins and either bankrupted and absorbed by the trust, or allowed to eke out bare survival. If you supplied coal to the railroad trust, all the railroads would refuse to buy your coal unless you knocked your prices down until you were making next to nothing—or losing money. Hell, if you got too frisky, they might refuse to carry your coal from the coal mine to the market, and then where'd you be?

Enter the trustbusters, led by Senator John Sherman, author of the 1890 Sherman Act, America's first antitrust law. In arguing for his bill, Sherman said to the Senate: "If we will not endure a King as a political power we should not endure a King over the production, transportation, and sale of the necessaries of life. If we would not submit to an emperor we should not submit to an autocrat of trade with power to prevent competition and to fix the price of any commodity."

In other words, when a company gained too much power, it became the same kind of kingly authority that the colonists overthrew in 1776. Government "by the people, of the people and for the people" was incompatible with concentrated corporate power from companies so large that they were able to determine how people lived their lives, made their incomes and structured their cities and towns.

This theory of antitrust is called the "harmful dominance" theory, and it worked. In the early part of the twentieth century, the largest commercial empires—such as John D. Rockefeller's Standard Oil Company—were shattered by the application of the Sherman Act. As time went by, other antitrust laws like the Clayton Act and the FTC Act reaffirmed the harmful dominance approach to antitrust: the idea that the law should protect the public, workers, customers and business owners from any harms resulting from excessive corporate power.

Not everybody liked this approach. Monopoly is a powerful and seductive idea. Starting a business often involves believing that you know something other people don't, that you can see something others can't see. Building that business up into a success only bolsters that view, proving that you possess the intellect, creativity and drive to create something others can't even conceive of.

In this light, competition seems wasteful: why must you expend resources fighting off copycats and pretenders when you could be using that same time delighting your customers and enriching your shareholders? As Peter Thiel puts it, "Competition is for losers."

The competition-is-for-losers set never let go of their dream of being autocrats of trade. They dreamt of a world where the invisible hand would tenderly lift them and set them down atop a throne of industry, from which they could direct the lives of millions of lesser beings who don't know what they want until a man of vision shows it to them.

These autocrats-in-waiting were already wealthy, and they bankrolled fringe kooks who had very different ideas about the correct administration of antitrust.

Chief among these was Robert Bork, who was best known for having served as Nixon's solicitor general, in which capacity he was complicit in a string of impeachable crimes against the American people, which led to his flunking his senate confirmation hearing, when Ronald Reagan tried to elevate him to the Supreme Court.

Bork had some *wild* ideas. He agreed with the autocrat set that the antitrust law *should* permit them to seize control over the nation, but then, so did a lot of weirdo Renfields who sucked up to capitalism's most powerful bloodsuckers.

What set Bork apart was his conviction that America's antitrust laws *already* celebrated monopolies as innately efficient and beneficial. According to Bork's theories, the existing antitrust statutes recognized that most monopolies were a great deal for "consumers," and that if we only read the statutes carefully enough, and reviewed the transcripts of the legislative debates in fine-enough detail, we'd see that Congress never set out to block companies from gaining enough power to become autocrats of trade—rather, they only wanted the law to step in when the autocrats abused their power to harm "consumers."

This is the "consumer welfare" standard, a theory as economically bankrupt as it is historically unsupportable. Let's be clear here: the plain language of America's antitrust laws makes it *very* clear that Congress wanted to block monopolies because it worried about the *concentration* of corporate power, not just the *abuse* of that power. This is inarguable: think of John Sherman stalking the floor of the Senate, railing against autocrats of trade, declaiming that "we should not endure a King over the production, transportation, and sale of the necessaries of life." These are not the statements of a man who liked most monopolies and merely sought to restrain the occasional monopolist who lost sight of his duty to make life better for the public.

Setting aside this fantastical alternate history, Bork's theories can sound plausible—at first. After all, if a company that buys up its suppliers or merges with its rivals can attain "economies of scale" and new efficiencies from putting all those businesses under one roof, then we, the consumers, might find ourselves enjoying lower prices and better products. Who wouldn't want that?

But "consumer" is only one of our aspects in society. We are also "workers," "parents," "residents" and, not least, "*citizens*." If our cheaper products come at the expense of our living wage, or the viability of our neighborhoods, or the democratically accountable authority of our elected representatives, have we *really* come out ahead?

"Consumer," is a truly undignified self-conception. To be a consumer is to be a mere ambulatory wallet, "voting with your dollars" to acquire life's comforts and necessities, without regard to the impact their production has on your neighborhood, your environment, your politics or your kids' futures.

Maybe you disagree. Maybe you find enormous pleasure in "retail therapy" and revel in the plethora of goods on offer, supply chains permitting. Maybe the idea of monopolists finding ways to deliver lower prices and higher quality matters more to you than the working conditions in the factories they emerged from or the character of your town's Main Street. Maybe you think that you might secretly be a Borkist.

Sorry, you're not a Borkist. Bork's conception of maximizing consumer welfare by lowering prices and increasing quality may sound like a straightforward policy. When a company merges with a rival or buys up a little upstart before it can become a threat, all a regulator has to do is ask, "Did this company raise prices or lower quality, or is it likely to do so?"

That does *sound* like a commonsense proposition, I grant you. But for Bork—and his co-conspirators at the far-right University of Chicago School of Economics—"consumer welfare" was no mere matter of watching to see whether prices rose after companies formed monopolies.

The Chicago School pointed out that sometimes prices go up for their own reasons: rises in the price of oil or other key inputs, say; or logistical snarls, foreign exchange fluctuations or rent hikes on key facilities. Good monopolies don't *want* to raise prices, they reasoned, so most of the time, when a monopolist raised their prices it would be because they were caught in a squeeze by rising costs. The last thing the government should do to these poor, beleaguered monopolists was kick them while they were down by accusing them of price gouging even as they were scrambling to get by during an oil crisis.

Of course, the Chicago Boys admitted, there were *some* bad monopolists out there, and *they* might raise prices just because they know they don't have to worry about competitors. The Chicago School used complicated mathematical models to sort the good monopolists from the bad ones.

These models were highly abstract and really only comprehensible to acolytes of the consumer welfare cult, who would produce them on demand—for a fee. If you ran a big business and wanted to merge with your main competitor, you could pay a Chicago School economist to build a model that would prove to the regulators at the DoJ and FTC that this would result in a *good* monopoly.

But say that after this good merger was approved, prices went up anyway? No problem: if the DoJ came calling, you could hire a Chicago School economist who'd whip up a new model, this one proving that all the price hikes were due to "exogenous factors" and not due to your price gouging.

No matter how large a post-merger company turned out to be, no matter how bald its post-merger shenanigans were, these

SEIZE THE MEANS OF COMPUTATION

economic models could absolve the company of any suspicion of wrongdoing. And since only Chicago-trained economists understood these models, no one could argue with their conclusions —especially not the regulators they were designed to impress.

Despite the superficial appeal of protecting "consumer welfare," this antitrust theory was obviously deficient: based on ahistorical fiction and contrary to the letter of the law and all the jurisprudence to date. Plus, the whole idea that the purpose of anti-monopoly law was to promote *good* monopolies was just ... daft.

But consumer welfare won. Monopolies have always had their fans, people who think that business leaders are Great Men of History, singular visionaries who have the power to singlehandedly revolutionize society and make us all better off if we just get out of their way and let them do their thing.

That's why they railed against "wasteful competition." Competition is wasteful because it wastes the time of these Ayn Rand heroes who could otherwise be focusing on delivering a better future for us all.

Unsurprisingly, some of the most ardent believers in this story are already rich. They are captured by the tautology of a providential society: "If I am rich, it must be because I am brilliant. How can you tell I'm brilliant? Well, for starters, I'm rich. Having proven my wealth and brilliance, it's clear that I should be in charge of things."

The Chicago School had deep-pocketed backers who kept them awash in money, even though their ideas were on the fringes. Chicago School archduke Milton Friedman described the movement's strategy:

"Only a crisis—actual or perceived—produces real change. When that crisis occurs, the actions that are taken depend on the ideas that are lying around. That, I believe, is our basic function: to develop alternatives to existing policies, to keep them alive and available until the politically impossible becomes the politically inevitable."

Friedman believed that if the movement could simply keep plugging, eventually a crisis would occur and its ideas would move from the fringes to the center. Friedman's financial backers agreed, and bankrolled the movement through its decades in the wilderness.

The oil crisis of the 1970s was the movement's opportunity. Energy shortages and inflation opened a space for a new radical politics, and around the world, a new kind of far-right leader took office; Ronald Reagan in the USA, Margaret Thatcher in the UK, Brian Mulroney in Canada.

Not all of the political revolutions of the 1970s were peaceful: Augusto Pinochet staged a coup in Chile, deposing elected president Salvador Allende, slaughtering 40,000 of his supporters, imprisoning 80,000 ordinary people in gulags, and torturing tens of thousands more. Pinochet was supported—financially, morally and militarily—by the democratically elected right-wing leaders and the Chicago School of Economics, who sent a delegation to Chile to help oversee the transformation of the country based on their "ideas lying around."

This global revolution marked the beginning of the neoliberal era, and with it, generations of policy that celebrated the ultra-rich as the ordained leaders of our civilization.

Throughout the neoliberal era, Bork's antitrust theories have dominated all over the world. The Chicago School's financial backers had invested wisely: the rise and rise of Chicago economics has shifted trillions in wealth to the already wealthy, while workers' wages stagnated, the middle class dwindled and millions of residents of the world's wealthiest countries slipped into poverty.

Bork's investors consolidated their gains. They sponsored economics chairs and whole economics departments and created the Manne Seminars, an annual junket in Florida, where federal judges were treated to luxury accommodations and "continuing education" workshops on Bork's unhinged theories.

Forty percent of the US federal judiciary graduated from the Manne Seminars, and empirical analysis of their rulings shows that they took Bork's consumer welfare theories to heart, consistently finding that monopolies were "efficient" and that mergers should be waved through and anticompetitive conduct forgiven.

Even the judges who *didn't* attend a Manne Seminar were captured by its influence: after more than forty years of Borkism, any judge, hearing any antitrust case, is briefed with decades' worth of precedent based on the consumer welfare theory.

Bork and his defenders assured us that decades of sustained monopolism would produce an incredible bounty for all: efficient, gigantic, vertically integrated firms offering goods and services at fantastically low prices, to the benefit of all.

They were half-right. Think back to that Open Markets Institute list of highly concentrated industries: *pharmaceuticals, health insurers, appliances, athletic shoes, defense contractors, book publishing, booze, drug stores, office supplies, eyeglasses, LCD glass, glass bottles, vitamin C, car parts, bottle caps, airlines, railroads, mattresses, Lasik lasers, cowboy boots and candy.*

Some of these industries did lower prices, at least some of the time. Some of the largest firms in these industries are "efficient"— in the sense of overcoming logistical challenges that would have been counted as fanciful in the days of Bork. Amazon fits both of those bills: cheap goods, delivered quickly.

But all of this comes at a price: the rise of "autocrats of trade": unelected princelings whose unaccountable whims dictate how we live, work, learn and play. Apple's moderators decide which apps you can use, and if they decline to list an educational game about sweatshop labor or an app that notifies you when a US drone kills a civilian overseas, well, that's that.

Google decides which search results we see—and which ones we don't. If Google doesn't prioritize a local business, it might fail—while Google's decision to feature a rival will make it a huge success. The same goes for newspapers, blogs and other sites—if Google downranks your newspaper, it effectively ceases to exist.

During the Covid lockdowns, Google colluded with review websites and app-based delivery services to trick people who wanted to order in their dinners. Search for your local restaurant on Google and you'd get a phone number for a scammy boiler room where low-wage workers would pretend to be staff at your local eatery and take your order. Then they'd call up the restaurant (they had the real number) and place your order with them. Restaurants that tried to maintain their own delivery staff and set their own prices and terms for delivery found themselves nonconsensually opted into predatory delivery apps.

Facebook decides which news you see—and which news you don't. If Facebook—or Instagram, or WhatsApp—kicks you off their platform, it can cost you your artistic career, or access to customers for your small business, or contact with your distant family, or the schedule and carpool for your kid's Little League games.

Microsoft, Airbnb, Uber, LinkedIn … the largest tech firms structure our lives in myriad ways, without regard to our well-being, without fear of competition and largely without regulation (for now).

Of course, brick-and-mortar is subject to a high degree of concentration and exercises enormous power over our lives, too. Back when all of American bookselling was collapsing into two chains—Borders and Barnes & Noble—the buyers for those chains held every writer's career in their hands. Just announcing that a writer's book sales were too low to warrant inclusion on either chain's shelves would trigger that writer's immediate defenestration by most publishers, or, if the writer had a *very* supportive editor, a career reboot under a pen name.

Borders is long gone today. Barnes & Noble is struggling. There's a scrappy independent bookselling trade, small stores run by committed booksellers who effectively take a vow of poverty to serve their communities—but they have to buy all their books from a *single* distributor, Ingram, who bought out their largest competitor, Baker & Taylor, in 2019. The power of two chain buyers to make or break a writer's career has been replaced by the power of one distributor to do so.

This is a microcosm for so many industries: Walmart crushed Main Street retail, then used its monopsony power to decide which products it would carry, and on what terms, driving some companies under by refusing to carry them, and others by insisting on discounts that the desperate companies ultimately couldn't afford.

But of course, all of this is just a sideshow compared to Amazon's effect on bookselling and all other forms of retail. The company's market power—captured by selling products at a loss for years, burning investor capital to force others out of business—is reinforced by its Prime program, which holds its best customers hostage to the $150/year sunk cost.

One company now has the power to wreck its workers' bodies (in many towns, Amazon is the only major employer); choke our streets with delivery vans; and ruin small businesses by inviting counterfeits or cloning their products. That same company decides which books are sold—either by refusing to carry them, or by ranking them low on search results.

Amazon is an enormously powerful autocrat of trade. In some ways, it is unexceptional: autocrats of trade wield similar power in the global shipping industry (controlled by just four firms), meatpacking (four firms) or baby formula (four companies).

But Amazon *is* different, as are Google, Apple, Microsoft, Salesforce, Uber, DoorDash, Facebook and the rest of the Big Tech stable.

They're different for two reasons: first, because they control the means of computation. These companies rule our digital world, the place where we find one another, form communities and mobilize in solidarity to take collective action. Winning tech back isn't more important than preventing runaway climate change or ending gender-based violence and discrimination, but it's hard to imagine how we'll do either—or anything else of significance—without digital infrastructure to hold us together.

Fixing tech isn't more important than fixing everything else, but unless we fix tech, we can forget about winning any of those other fights.

Second, tech is built on digital computers and networks, those strange hyper-objects I described in the introduction. For all that our computers take on many forms—blenders, watches, phones, cars, airplanes, thermostats—they are all, at root, functionally equivalent.

The modern computer went from a specialized instrument of giant companies, militaries and governments to a ubiquitous, invisible part of our social fabric in just a few decades. The mechanism behind this explosive growth is intimately connected to the deep nature of computers.

Before World War II, we didn't have computers—we had electromechanical tabulating engines, giant machines designed to solve a single kind of problem, like calculating a ballistics table or an actuarial table for an insurance company.

Turing's breakthrough—well, *one* of Turing's breakthroughs (well, one of the breakthroughs by Turing and the exiled Polish mathematicians and British boffins at Bletchley Park)—was to conceptualize and refine the *universal* computer: a gadget that could run *any* program, provided it was expressed in valid symbolic logic (a collection of "valid symbolic logic" is also known as "a computer program").

Across the Atlantic, John von Neumann (and a collection of exiled Hungarian mathematicians, as well as assorted brilliant people at the Princeton Institute) created and built the first "von Neumann machine"—a physical instantiation of a Universal Turing Machine.

The rest, as they say, was history. The universality of the general-purpose computer was both profound and powerful. Any computer can run any program we can write, but slower computers with less memory might take a *very* long time to execute it. The hand-built computers assembled by von Neumann and his team (and their kids: the children of the Princeton Institute's fellows were pressed into service over their summer breaks, made to hand-wind copper wire around insulators to form the first memory cores) might take millions of years to boot up a copy of Photoshop. But, given enough time and enough electricity—and enough maintenance—boot it up they will. Eventually.

Lots of people set out to make computers a little faster or a little cheaper, hoping to solve a problem that mattered to them or some other engineering or record-keeping challenge. Every time they succeeded, everyone else who was using computers to solve their own problems got the benefit of that breakthrough, as their own problems got faster and cheaper to solve.

What's more, as computers got faster and cheaper, the range of problems they could cost-effectively solve expanded. Each improvement in computers added to the pool of people who were using computers and trying to improve them. A computing improvement driven by a desire to process astronomy data made it easier to model floodplains, and also to send email, and also to animate sprites in a video game.

Universality created an army of partisans, all fighting for better computers. They wanted faster, cheaper computers for different reasons, but they all wanted faster, cheaper computers. Because computers were universal, they moved into every industrial sector, every field of artistic endeavor, every form of leisure, every scientific discipline.

This collective demand for better computers justified unimaginably vast R&D expenditures, whose triumphs were faster, cheaper computers that found their way into still more corners of our lives. This is what "software is eating the world" really means: the positive externalities of computer improvements set up a virtuous cycle where improvements begat partisans for still more improvements, which created still more partisans.

Universality isn't just a happy feature we've engineered into our computers: it's an inescapable part of their nature. It would be great if we could design a computer that could only run some programs: for example, if we could invent a printer (which is just a computer hooked up to a system for spraying ink on paper) that could only run the "print documents" program and not the "be infected with a virus that metastasizes across the network and infects all the PCs on it" program.

But we can't. Our printers are universal computers, and so are our thermostats and smart watches and cars.

All of this is to explain how computers are, indeed, exceptional. Computers are exceptional because they are universal, and that inescapable universal characteristic means that they have intrinsically low switching costs.

That may sound very highfalutin and technical. Admittedly, it requires a grasp of technical concepts from both economics and computer science. But it's not that complicated, as you'll see from this example of how these two principles saved Apple from destruction in the early 2000s.

Back then, Apple had a problem. Microsoft, a convicted monopolist, had a 95 percent share of the desktop operating system through its Windows product. Microsoft exploited that operating system monopoly to win a similar monopoly with productivity tools: the Microsoft Office suite consisting of Word, Excel and PowerPoint.

Microsoft had long since clobbered all the other Windows productivity programs through dirty tricks: as the old internal company motto had it, "DOS isn't done until Lotus won't run." Lotus 1-2-3 was an early spreadsheet program and a major competitor to Microsoft Excel; it was well understood that Microsoft tweaked its new operating system releases so that people who upgraded would no longer be able to launch Lotus 1-2-3 and would have to wait until a new version was released that coped with the new incompatibilities Microsoft introduced.

That meant that nearly everyone who used a computer used Windows, and nearly everyone who used Windows used Microsoft Office.

That was a big problem for Apple.

Back then, I was a kind of itinerant Chief Information Officer, building and managing networks for small and medium-sized companies. Most of the computers I managed were PCs running Windows, but a few of my users—the designers and sometimes the CEOs—used Macs.

These Mac users' colleagues needed to collaborate with them on word processor files, spreadsheets and slideshows created in Microsoft Office. They'd send them over—on removable disks, or using internal email or file transfers—and the Mac users would open them using Microsoft Office for MacOS.

Or at least, they'd *try* to open them. Office for the Mac was a *terrible* piece of software. Much of the time, it wouldn't be able to read the files sent by Windows users—and vice versa, as files saved out of the Mac version of Office would be rejected by Office for Windows as "corrupted."

This was a pain in the ass for me and my users, but it was a nightmare for Apple, because the way I dealt with this—the way thousands of IT managers like me dealt with it—was to buy new PCs for my designers and stick them on their desks next to their Macs. These PCs were dedicated Office workstations.

But that was a lot of work, and eventually those designers—and even those CEOs—agreed that two computers was one too many. I beefed up the graphics cards in the Windows users' machines, installed Adobe Photoshop and QuarkXpress for Windows, and got rid of their Macs altogether.

Apple knew this was happening, and understood that it was a deliberate strategy. Apple founder and CEO Steve Jobs had a solution: he tasked some of his technical staff with reverse engineering Microsoft Office and creating a rival product called iWork, which consisted of three programs—Pages, Numbers and Keynote—that could read and write the files created by Microsoft's Word, Excel and PowerPoint.

At that instant, everything changed. Mac users no longer had to forfeit the ability to collaborate with the Windows users, who accounted for 95 percent of the computing world, as a condition of using an Apple product. Instead, they attained seamless interoperability—their files Just Worked for Windows users, and Windows users' files Just Worked for them.

And once iWork was in the world, Microsoft users suddenly entered a new reality: they could give up Windows and buy Macs and take all their files with them, and those files would Just Work, too.

You see, Microsoft had network effects on its side, and it used them to get big. Every Windows user was an Office user, and every Office user produced documents that other people wanted to read, edit and collaborate on. Every Office document created was another reason to become a Windows user, another file that you could potentially learn from, edit and improve. Every Windows user created more Office documents.

The corollary was that *leaving* the Windows world for a Mac was *very* costly indeed. Your own files would struggle to make the transition with you—many would be forever unreadable. The 95 percent of the computing world who were Windows users would struggle to collaborate with you, thanks to Microsoft's terrible Mac software.

Even if you didn't like Windows, even if you preferred the Mac, there were billions of reasons to stick with Microsoft's products—billions of users, and trillions of documents.

Microsoft used network effects to build a winner-take-all system that sucked in new users and shackled them to its platform with high switching costs. If Microsoft's monopoly had been on some physical product—say, a proprietary lightbulb screw, or a proprietary way of connecting attachments to kitchen mixers—then that might have been the end of the story.

After all, even if you're a skilled machinist who can make

adapters to plug your proprietary mixer attachments into a rival's mixer, that only solves *your* problem. Your neighbor is still stuck buying a Microsoft mixer in order to preserve their investment in attachments.

But software is different. It is universal. Tech is exceptional.

The fact that all computers are universal, all capable of running every program, meant that there would *always* be a way to write a Mac program that could read and write Microsoft Office files better than Microsoft Office for Mac could. And once that program existed in the world, it could be given away or sold to anyone who had a Mac and an internet connection.

If you're a Computer User of a Certain Age, you know what happened next. Apple launched a cheeky, ballsy ad campaign called "Switch," which featured Windows users who'd ditched Microsoft and bought Macs, extolling the simplicity of reading and writing their files with iWork, praising the ease of collaborating with Windows users who hadn't made the switch (yet). From my perspective as an IT professional, who, at the time, was writing purchase orders for millions of dollars' worth of workplace computers every year, iWork saved Apple.

Microsoft used network effects to get big, and used high switching costs to stay big. Once Apple lowered those switching costs, the network effects no longer mattered so much—indeed, they became a double-edged sword. Every person who got stuck inside Microsoft's walled garden was a reason for others to join —but every person who *escaped* that walled garden became a reason for others to leave, too.

Remember, there was nothing *technical* Microsoft could have done to prevent Apple from reverse engineering its files and making iWork. The deep universality of computers meant that Apple would always be able to blow a hole in Microsoft's walled garden.

Which is not to say that Microsoft didn't *try*. The old Office file formats were a notoriously gnarly hairball of obfuscation and cruft. Even Microsoft struggled to maintain compatibility with all the different versions of Office it had pushed out over the decades.

But here's the kicker: after Apple successfully launched iWork,

Microsoft *gave up*. It stopped obfuscating Office, and instead, took those Office file formats to a multistakeholder standardization body, and helped create an open, public standard for reading and writing Office files. Today, that standard is everywhere: Google Docs, LibreOffice, iWork, Office and a million websites that can ingest your Office files and turn them into something that lives on the internet.

The consumer welfare standard led to industrial concentration across the board, so in that regard, tech is *not* exceptional. But tech *is* exceptional in that it is intrinsically interoperable, which means that we can use interop to make Big Tech a lot smaller, very quickly—we can attack network effects by reducing switching costs.

Making it easier for technology users—everyone—to leave Big Tech platforms for smaller tech created by co-ops, nonprofits, tinkerers and startups will hasten the day that we can bring Big Tech to heel in other ways. Siphoning off Big Tech's users means reducing its revenues, which are otherwise fashioned into lobbying tools.

It also robs Big Tech of its partisans—for example, the small businesses who stand up for Amazon even though it is slowly destroying them, because they can't reach their customers without it. If they could leave Amazon but still reach its customers, they'd stop telling lawmakers to leave poor Amazon alone.

Finally, it will trigger an exodus of Big Tech's most valuable resource: its technical workforce. Techies are in demand and can exploit that bargaining power to command high wages and perks, but Big Tech's takeover has substantially dampened techies' dreams of starting their own rival businesses where they don't have to answer to a manager. Interop means that you can quit your awful Facebook job and create a rival service that plugs into Facebook, providing a nonexploitative alternative for the users you signed on to help.

Starved of cash, allies and engineers, Big Tech will be a soft target for other, stiffer forms of regulation, like breakups. Starved of cash, Big Tech will struggle to buy up the small competitors that could someday grow to pose a threat to them.

Tech is exceptional because digital computers and networks are universal, and universal things are interoperable, and interoperability lowers switching costs. Monopoly is an elephant, and you eat an elephant one bite at a time. For all these reasons, I think tech should be antitrust's first bite.

But that's not the only way that tech is exceptional. Our digital tools aren't just how corporations and governments surveil and control us—they're also how we form communities and coordinate our tactics to fight back.

If we someday triumph over labor exploitation, gender discrimination and violence, colonialism and racism, and snatch a habitable planet from the jaws of extractive capitalism, it will be thanks to technologically enabled organizing. From street protests to mutual aid funds, from letter-writing to organizing sit-ins, from blockades to strikes, we *need* digital networks to prosecute our struggle.

That is the other way that tech is exceptional. The fight for a free, fair and open digital future isn't more important than any of those other fights, but it is *foundational*. Tech is the terrain on which our future fights will be fought. If we can't seize the means of computation, we will lose the fight before it is even joined.

2

Network Effects vs. Switching Costs

The history of technology is one long guerrilla fight where the established giants wield network effects against scrappy upstarts whose asymmetrical warfare weapon of choice is low switching costs.

Take the early web. Actually, the early *pre*-web. Almost a decade before Tim Berners-Lee—then a researcher at the CERN supercollider in Switzerland—created the World Wide Web, academics at the University of Minnesota had launched the first "user-friendly" way to access the internet: a service called *gopher*.

Before gopher, the internet was a motley, mismatched set of connected servers at universities, research institutions and military and government institutes all around the world. Each internet node had its own servers, offering their own services: one might let you search the catalogs of its library, another might tell you the local weather, a third might have a file-server full of technical manuals.

There was no central directory of these services. That was a feature, not a bug. The internet was designed to be a "network of networks"—a way for anyone to connect any kind of computer and make it accessible to anyone else. To add a new service to the internet, you designed it, built it, and plugged it in (after cajoling your university's IT administrators for an IP address and a network connection). There was no way to know what was plugged into the internet because there was no way to control what was plugged into the internet.

Just finding out what was on the internet was one challenge, but even when you found a service you wanted to use, you still had to figure out how to use it. These early services were all accessed and controlled via a terminal program (or, indeed, an actual, physical terminal—a kind of brainless printer/keyboard or screen/keyboard device from the computational Paleolithic age). Each one had its own esoteric syntax—abbreviated commands with finicky spellings and variables that had to be appended in just the right order, with just the right separators. To "browse" the internet in those days, you had to master dozens of esoteric computing environments.

Enter gopher. Gopher was created in 1991 by a team at the University of Minnesota's Microcomputer Center—the group that supported students who wanted to hook their computers up to the internet. This was a significant challenge! The Microcomputer Center staff had to guide students through installing the basic networking software that let their computers send and receive internet protocol messages (in those days, most PCs shipped with operating systems that were not capable of connecting to the internet out of the box).

On top of that, the Microcomputer Center had to install specialized software—an email program; a "newsreader" for reading Usenet, the internet's message boards; a program for transferring files; and more—for each student and show them how to use it.

But most of all, the Microcomputer Center had to teach students and faculty how to use the finicky command-line services that constituted the bulk of the internet's servers. Many of these ran homebrewed server programs that were unique to their institutions, reflecting the idiosyncratic views of the systems' administrators about the best way of using the data they maintained. The hours you put into learning one system wouldn't transfer over to the next.

That's where gopher came in. The Microcomputer Center's programmers created intermediate programs that served as a kind of overlay to each of these one-off systems. These programs would present naïve users with numbered menus listing all the commands the system supported. Instead of remembering that typing "ls" produces a list of files from an ftp server (a kind of early file-server), you just looked down a menu like this:

List files
Get file
Delete file
Upload file

It was a lot easier to type "1." than it was to remember "ls," and while it took a fair bit of work to create these menuing overlays, the gopher programmers only had to do this once for each service, and then they could train the users they supported to use menus, rather than teaching each user a hundred obscure computing dialects.

Gopher menus didn't just let you interact with a service—they also let you hop from one service to another, the way modern web-pages today do. Gopher became both a directory of nearly everything connected to the internet and a means of connecting to and controlling all those services.

Gopher was an open protocol. Any programmer who wanted to help other people interact with a service for which there was no menuing system could write their own, and make it available in "gopherspace."

In this way, hundreds of proprietary interfaces designed for highly technical users, many of them the product of the world's largest technology companies, were commodified, subsumed into a volunteer-managed, globe-spanning interface that was designed to welcome laypeople to the burgeoning internet. Though some service operators objected to these unsolicited improvements, they had few options: they could send angry lawyer letters, re-engineer their systems to break gopher automation tools, or make their public services private, with access gated by passwords.

Most of these services did nothing, apart from grumble. Some sent lawyer letters, but the law was unsettled and confusing, and much of the time, the recipients of these letters simply ignored them (or not—gopher developers built their automation tools because they *liked* the services they were trying to make accessible, so a letter from the services' maintainers explaining that they didn't welcome these volunteer efforts was sometimes enough to stop them).

For a brief moment, gopher was the dominant internet service. The World Wide Web was *much* smaller than gopher, and, unlike gopher, the web grew primarily through the creation of new websites—services designed for the web. Gopher, by contrast, grew by swallowing existing services.

What happened next? It's the best part. As the web's growth took off, web users tired of having to remember which services they accessed via gopher and which ones they accessed via the web. Gopher's developers tried to solve this by making it possible to load webpages in a gopher browser, but the web's developers turned the tables on them, making it possible to load *gopher* pages in *web* browsers.

Gopher simply became another kind of webpage, which you accessed by typing *gopher://* rather than *http://* into your location bar. The administrators who ran gopher servers stood up webservers alongside them, accessing the same documents, so you could type either *gopher://* or *http://* and have an identical experience.

Gopher dwindled and disappeared (try to remember the last time *you* typed *gopher://*). But the collapse of gopher wasn't the end of gopherspace. The files, services and sites that we once accessed with gopher are now part of the web.

The gopher story is remarkable because it's such a perfect tale of how the intrinsic interoperability of technology meant that cornering the market on digital systems was a technical impossibility. It didn't matter that the largest corporations in the world created mainframe-based walled gardens; volunteers were able to open them up with hobby projects.

Technology is so flexible that even as gopher was swallowing the web—integrating http and HTML into gopher browsers— the web was swallowing gopher, too. It's like one of those weird Wikipedia pages like "lakes with islands" that list lakes that have islands.

Again and again in the early days of personal computing and the web, we get stories like this. Take the IBM PC: IBM was a giant, abusive tech monopoly long before this was in vogue. The company was tightly integrated with the US military and government, and this afforded it a measure of security; even though its rivals griped to their members of Congress about how they were being bigfooted by IBM, the company fended off serious regulatory action for decades, thanks to powerful friends in the Pentagon and other parts of the US state apparatus.

Eventually, IBM's luck ran out. In 1970, the DoJ opened an antitrust case into "Big Blue" (the company's army of sales reps all wore blue ties). Because IBM was a monopoly it had a lot of money to spend in the ensuing fight. A *lot* of money. Over the next twelve years, IBM outspent the *entire Department of Justice Antitrust Division*, every year, in a war that came to be called "antitrust's Vietnam."

IBM won. Sorta. Twelve years later, the Reagan administration decided to drop the enforcement action against Big Blue (they broke up AT&T instead—for the ideologues in Reagan's orbit, AT&T was an acceptable antitrust target because it was so entwined with the US government that breaking it up was like making the government smaller).

But now, IBM lost. Twelve years of having to produce every memo and the minutes of every meeting took its toll. Running a company where every word committed to paper—let alone uttered in public—had to be vetted by paranoid lawyers locked in a high-stakes battle with the US government changed IBM, blunted its predatory instincts.

The company began to second-guess its commercial plans, steering clear of the kinds of things that the DoJ frowned upon. The DoJ didn't like it when a big company monopolized the parts for its products, so IBM made a PC that used commodity parts— parts that any manufacturer could buy on the open market.

Nor did the DoJ like it when companies tied their software to their hardware, so IBM decided not to make its own PC operating system. IBM chairman John Opel asked a friend who served with him on the board of the United Way if she knew anyone who could provide an OS for his company's PC. Her name was Mary Gates, and her son, Bill Gates, had a company that fit the bill: Micro-Soft. (They dropped the hyphen later.)

Once the IBM PC—built from commodity components, running a third-party operating system—hit the market, other manufacturers wanted to follow it. They could buy their operating

systems from Microsoft and their parts from IBM's suppliers—
but they still needed a "ROM"—the "read-only memory" chip
that had the low-level code that made a PC a PC.

In stepped Phoenix Computers, a small startup, who reverse
engineered the PC ROM and made its own, customizing it as
needed for a booming market in "PC clones"—Compaq, Dell,
Gateway and even electronics giants like Sony.

Here we see two kinds of interoperability in action. IBM
"voluntarily" embraced interoperable components and operating
systems—that is, the DoJ didn't order it to do these things, but
twelve years of brutal legal battles convinced IBM not to stir up
the DoJ's hornet's nest again.

But alongside that voluntary interop, we have *adversarial*
interop, wherein engineers at a scrappy startup pitted their wits
against the best minds at the world's largest and most powerful technology company—and won, cloning the PC ROM and
selling it on the open market (something IBM likely tolerated due
to the possibility of attracting more DoJ attention if it clobbered
a small company that was enabling rivals to launch competing
products).

Today, IBM *no longer makes PCs*. Interoperability in PCs
meant that anyone who started on an IBM PC could switch to
a Compaq or a Gateway or a Sony. Interoperability also means
that anyone who makes that leap can leap again—to a Mac,
where iWork will let them open and save all those Microsoft
Office documents they created on their IBM PCs, Compaqs and
Gateways.

And that's without even getting into free/open operating
systems like GNU/Linux, available in dozens of flavors, all of
which can run on Apple hardware or hardware from any of the
PC vendors. Free GNU/Linux apps like LibreOffice can open the
files created by Microsoft Office and iWork and Google Docs,
and exchange them seamlessly with users of rival platforms.

That seamlessness in Office documents isn't just a matter
of diligent reverse engineering. Remember, after the success of
Apple's iWork, Microsoft threw in the towel and ceded control
over the Office file formats to an independent standards body,
which means that anyone who knows how to write software

can download a copy of the standard and the reference code for implementing it, and make their own Office product that will work with everyone else's.

Walled gardens can only exist when switching costs are high. Tech companies understand that making interoperability-proof computers is a lost cause—like making dry water. Computers work *because* they are interoperable.

The outcome of a war on general-purpose computers that is fought on a technological battlefield is foreordained. General-purpose computers will win every time.

But would-be tech monopolists (and their investors) still dream of walled gardens and scheme to build them.

In June 2021, a US federal court dealt a severe blow to the FTC's antitrust complaint against Facebook, rejecting the regulator's case. But the court left the door open to a new complaint, inviting the FTC to re-file its case.

In August 2021, the FTC did just that, filing an "amended complaint," guided by the new FTC Chair Lina Khan, who is also the leading theorist of Big Tech and antitrust. The new complaint drew heavily on the documents that Facebook had been forced to cough up in the earlier case, and large parts of the filing were initially blacked out for reasons of commercial confidentiality.

But by October 2021, the FTC had won the right to unseal many of its new documents, and that's where we learned some of the grimy details of Facebook's plans to raise switching costs. Over and over again, the FTC found senior Facebook managers and product designers explicitly designing products so that users would suffer if they left Facebook for a rival.

Take this quote from a memo that Facebook's Mergers and Acquisitions department sent to CEO Mark Zuckerberg, giving the case for acquiring a company that let users upload and share their photos:

> *imo, photos (along with comprehensive/smart contacts and unified messaging) is perhaps one of the most important ways we can make switching costs very high for users—if we are where all users' photos reside because the upoading [sic] (mobile and web), editing, organizing, and sharing features are best in class, will be*

very tough for a user to switch if they can't take those photos and associated data/comments with them.

Later, a Facebook engineer discusses the plan to reduce interoperability selectively, based on whether a Facebook app developer might help people use rivals to its own projects:

[S]o we are literally going to group apps into buckets based on how scared we are of them and give them different APIs? How do we ever hope to document this? Put a link at the top of the page that says "Going to be building a messenger app? Click here to filter out the APIs we won't let you use!" And what if an app adds a feature that moves them from 2 to 1? Shit just breaks? And a messaging app can't use Facebook login? So the message is, "if you're going to compete with us at all, make sure you don't integrate with us at all."? I am just dumbfounded… [T]hat feels unethical somehow, but I'm having difficulty explaining how. It just makes me feel like a bad person.

Then, a Facebook executive describes how switching costs are preventing Google's "Google+" service from gaining users:

[P]eople who are big fans of G+ are having a hard time convincing their friends to participate because 1/there isn't [sic] yet a meaningful differentiator from Facebook and 2/ switching costs would be high due to friend density on Facebook.

These are the machinations of a company that believes that its most profitable user-retention strategy is to lock its users up. They're the machinations of a company that is thoroughly uninterested in being better than its competitors—rather, they're dedicated to ensuring that leaving Facebook behind is so punishing and unpleasant that people stay, *even if they hate Facebook*.

Facebook isn't alone in realizing that winning user loyalty by providing an excellent experience is harder work than punishing disloyal users, nor are its user-facing services the only place where this strategy is deployed.

Many people have observed that Facebook's customers aren't

the users who socialize on its platform, but the advertisers who pay to reach those users. "If you're not paying for the product, you're the product" is often invoked to explain why Facebook treats its users so badly.

But being Facebook's customer—an advertiser or even a publisher—doesn't mean you'll get better treatment from the company. Time and again, the company has been caught stealing from advertisers, falsifying its records about who it showed their ads to, and for how long. At least half of the ads that companies pay Facebook to show to its users aren't actually seen by a human being—but Facebook bills the advertisers for that money anyway.

The same goes for the publishers whose commercially prepared reporting, opinion and coverage are a major reason that Facebook users are attracted to the platform. In 2015, Facebook decided to use these publishers as part of its bid to dethrone Google's YouTube service as the leading video platform online.

The result—the notorious "pivot to video"—was a devastating fraud, a mass-extinction event for media companies. Facebook lied to media companies about the popularity of Facebook videos, falsely claiming that Facebook users had all but abandoned reading text in favor of watching videos. They told the same lies to advertisers, whom they fraudulently billed for phantom ads that never ran on videos that were never watched. Media companies around the world fired their print journalists and built out expensive video production divisions.

This was Facebook's version of "fake it until you make it." The company *wanted* to be the number-one internet video platform, so it declared that it already *was* that platform, and suckered advertisers and media companies into participating in its delusion.

This is just a slightly sleazier version of what other companies had done before—think of Steve Jobs promising media companies that if they invested in making apps for his new iPad they would reap massive profits, tapping into a new movement in which readers were willing to "pay for content."

Jobs had no idea if Apple users would pay for apps, but he won either way: if media companies filled his App Store with software, then other software developers would follow, and some of them would eventually make apps that his customers valued, which would sell more iPads—even if no one was willing to pay for the news.

And if people *were* willing to pay for the news, well, Apple would be able to rake off 30 percent of the sale price of the app (and, once companies had completed their "pivot to apps," Jobs altered the deal, to guarantee Apple 30 percent of the app's sale price—and of all the purchases users made within the app; that is, the entire lifetime revenue of every app-using customer these companies had).

Apple's bet paid off. Users were willing to pay for apps—not as much as Jobs promised, but there were success stories like the *New York Times* that Apple could gesture toward when smaller newspapers complained that they'd spent all their available cash flow building an app that no one wanted to pay to use.

But Steve Jobs's famed "reality-distortion field" did not materialize for Mark Zuckerberg. Despite Facebook's egregious lies about the popularity of video on its platform, despite the billions media companies poured into video production based on those lies, despite Facebook's content-recommendation algorithms putting their fists on the scales to ensure that every user's feed was a wall of Facebook videos, Facebook users just *didn't want video*.

When the dust settled, advertisers lost the hundreds of millions they spent on ads that no one ever saw. Media companies had no way to service the debt or satisfy the investors that supplied the capital for their pivot to video. Worse, they had laid off their newsrooms and replaced them with video producers—many lured away from stable jobs with huge cash promises based on Facebook's fake video viewership numbers.

Even after laying off their video producers, these media companies couldn't recover. For one thing, they had jettisoned the staff and contract writers they'd need to pivot back to text, and even if they could get the band back together, they had blown through so much money on videos for an imaginary audience that they didn't have anything left to pay these writers.

Media companies *imploded*. The industry shed hundreds of jobs—young, promising creators at the start of their careers met with ruin, and many old veterans exited the field in ignominy, unable to find another job.

The idea that Facebook abuses its users because they're not its customers is just wrong. It treats its customers terribly. It also treats its workers abysmally—think of the traumatized army of content moderators whom Facebook puts to work in the content mines, screening images and videos of torture, sexual abuse, murder and other things they'll never un-see.

Facebook treats you terribly, but that's not because you're not its customer. They treat you terribly because they treat everyone terribly. They're a monstrous company.

It may seem like I'm picking on Facebook, and in truth, I am. All the tech giants are pretty terrible, but I'd argue that Facebook is uniquely bad.

Below is a two-dimensional grid. The x-axis is "more control-freaky." That's how much a company tries to circumscribe what you do and rob you of your technological self-determination. The y-axis is "more surveillant"—how much a company spies on you.

Google occupies the top left corner. The company is comparatively cavalier about exercising control over your behavior, because it spies on you and hems you in on all sides with its products. Google doesn't have to block its rivals from showing up in your searches. All it has to do is put its own services at the top of the page.

Now, Apple is in the bottom right corner. It doesn't care to spy on you, but then again, it doesn't need to: it can control you by depriving you of choice. Buy an iPhone and Apple gets to decide which apps you can use. Not content with burying its rivals on page umpty-million of its App Store results, Apple prohibits those

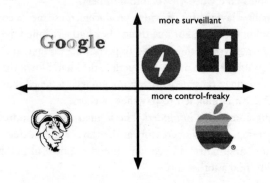

rivals from offering competing apps unless they cough up a 30 percent commission on every dime you spend, *and* it prevents you from installing apps unless they come from its App Store.

Finally, there's Facebook, up there in the top right corner: maximum surveillance, maximum control. It's a company that combines Google's insatiable appetite for your private data with Apple's iron-fisted control over how you use its service. The worst of all possible worlds.

What's more, Facebook has become the template for other tech giants, like TikTok. In fact, our 2x2 surveillance/control grid needs to get a lot bigger to accommodate TikTok, because it's so far off to the top right that I've had to put it on the top right corner of the last page of this book to get the scale right ... go ahead and check!

(Attentive readers will notice that there's a missing quadrant in this grid—the bottom left corner, where there is no surveillance *and* no control; that's the quadrant where community-supported, free/open software lives; more on that later.)

You don't have to agree that Facebook is worse than Google or Apple to know that something needs to be done about Big Tech. Digital technology was sold to us as an infinitely customizable, responsive, idiosyncratic new way of living. Networked tools were supposed to give us more control over our lives. Instead, we find ourselves manipulated, controlled, corralled and milked dry.

What is to be done?

3

Copyright Wars, Cybercrime, Terrorism, Human Trafficking and Other Gifts to Big Tech

The answer to the machine isn't the machine.

Everything policymakers have done to rein in Big Tech has only cemented the dominance of the handful of rotten companies who stole the internet from us.

Take the copyright wars. These really kicked off in earnest with Napster, the first mass-adopted peer-to-peer file-sharing platform. As a reminder, here's how Napster worked: Napster users installed the software and told it where they kept the digital music on their own computers. The Napster program contacted Napster's servers and uploaded a list of all the music that user had, which went into a master index of all the music available on all Napster users' computers.

To find music, you searched that index. I had just moved away from my hometown when Napster hit, and I spent a lot of time in hotel rooms and a small apartment in San Francisco searching for the obscure Toronto bands I'd grown up on, whose music I had only ever owned on the cassettes and vinyl EPs the bands had sold directly to fans at their gigs.

Each search was a roll of the dice. If I was lucky, a fan of the band would be online, with a collection of music they'd painstakingly digitized from a record album or cassette (this was a complex technical feat in those days). When my search found such a fellow traveler, I could open up their whole music collection, sorted by artist or album, and grab other treasures. I discovered some of my favorite bands this way: when someone has the same taste in obscure bands as you, the stuff they like that you haven't heard of has a high probability of being the music that you'll love, too.

Best of all was Napster's chat function, which allowed users to strike up conversations while these file exchanges were underway. As a Napster user, you could see who was downloading music from your collection, and which music they were ganking. This led to a lot of delightful conversations with fellow superfans of obscure Toronto bands, reminiscing about the shows we'd both been to, trading tips about what the band's members had gone on to next and every other topic.

Napster was great. At the time, it was the fastest-adopted technology in world history, beating out the DVD player. It emerged at a time when the record labels were in the midst of waves of anticompetitive mergers (presaging the merger mania that would shortly grip tech). The recording industry had enjoyed a series of windfalls based on format shifts, reselling fans the music they had on vinyl as cassette tapes, and then again as CDs. They felt entitled to resell those fans their music collections again, as digital files.

But the fans weren't biting. Having dabbled with home taping (and watched as the record industry conspicuously failed to collapse despite a litany of home-taping-is-killing-music complaints) music listeners quickly discovered the joys of "ripping" CDs (converting their music to MP3s) and burning them—so much so that Apple launched a major ad campaign whose slogan, "Rip, Mix, Burn," attracted the ire of the record industry.

No one was particularly bothered by what the record industry thought, though. Not only had the industry discredited itself with years of scare stories about home taping, but also Napster emerged at a time when the vast majority of recorded music was not available for sale on any official media (some estimates at the time put the figure at 80 percent). The record industry may have billed itself as the steward of the world's music heritage, but it had decided—for purely self-interested, commercial reasons—

to render nearly all of that heritage effectively unavailable, relegating it to used record bins and library shelves.

Napster, on the other hand, put all of that music back into fans' hands, in a matter of months. The company's users *loved* its service, and not (just) because the music was free. The company's surveys found that the majority of its users were willing to pay $15 per month for ongoing access to it, and they offered any reasonable licensing fee that the record industry would accept for legitimizing this arrangement.

Instead of accepting billions of dollars from music fans, the record industry sued. The courts were sympathetic to its copyright claims, and Napster was shortly extinct. What's more, the record industry's legal tactics ensured that Napster-like services found it hard, and soon impossible, to find investment (the record industry lawsuits named Napster's investors, and *their* investors, as parties to the suit, which seriously spooked venture capitalists and their backers).

But P2P refused to die, because nothing the record industry had to offer could come close to replacing it. The post-Napster P2P services designed themselves to be litigation-proof, so that they could exercise less control and oversight over their users and their listening habits.

The legal thinking went, "If our services have non-infringing uses, and if we can't eliminate the infringing ones, the courts will find that we have a right to operate." It was a reasonable theory, grounded in the landmark copyright-and-technology case of the twentieth century: *Betamax*.

Betamax (formally *Sony Corp. of America v. Universal City Studios, Inc.*) was a high-stakes lawsuit over the legality of home videocassette recorders, a case that ran from 1976 to 1984, when the Supreme Court ruled that VCRs were, indeed, legal.

The film industry's argument was that VCRs should be prohibited because they could be used to infringe copyright merely by recording a Hollywood movie off your cable or TV antenna, or by bringing that recording to a friend's house for a viewing party, or by making a copy.

Sony—the manufacturer of the Betamax, the first commercial home VCR technology—countered that there were *substantial non-infringing uses* for the VCR. For example, you could record congressional debate off C-SPAN (works by the US government are not copyrightable) or an old public domain movie off late-night TV. You also might record a copyrighted work but for a purpose that fits into one of copyright's "limitations and exceptions," which include "fair use" (a wide swath of uses that can be made of copyrighted works even if the copyright holder objects).

The studios countered by claiming that fair use was so limited that almost nothing you did with a VCR would qualify. They also pointed out that Sony had advertised its VCR for uses that were arguably copyright infringements, like recording Hollywood movies off of cable TV and then bringing them to a friend's house for a viewing party.

The Supreme Court found in Sony's favor. It didn't matter that the majority of VCR uses were infringing. It didn't even matter that Sony had told its customers that they should buy VCRs in order to infringe copyright. The fact that the VCR was "capable of sustaining a substantial non-infringing use" was all that mattered (in reality, what probably mattered more was the prevalence of VCRs by 1984, the year the Supremes ruled—there were six million VCRs in America's living rooms by then, and video-rental stores in nearly every town; the justices knew that if they banned the VCR, they'd seem out-of-touch and lose legitimacy, inviting the public to view them as nine dotards in robes. This was the 1980s, when Supreme Court justices still cared about whether the American public acknowledged their legitimacy).

The VCR was legalized, and though the Betamax itself lost out to the far more popular VHS format, the "Betamax rule" outlived both technologies: so long as a tool is capable of sustaining a substantial non-infringing use, it is legal.

(Just a side note here: the Betamax was a better VCR than the VHS. Its tapes were more reliable and produced a better image and sound. But the VHS was interoperable—anyone could build one—while the Betamax was a patented Sony creation, and off-limits to any rival. The lack of interop for Betamaxes killed the technology, but Sony's eight years' worth of legal adventures ensured that the rival VHS could operate without being sued into oblivion.)

Napster's successors believed the *Betamax* principle was on their side. They were right. Tools like Kazaa and Grokster had lots of "substantial non-infringing uses." Lots of musicians *wanted* their music distributed for free; many old public domain recordings were available on these networks, and the P2P tools that supported file formats beyond MP3 had all kinds of non-infringing material: ebooks of the Bible and fan-readings of Mark Twain novels and, yes, CSPAN videos of congressional hearings (including congressional hearings on the scourge of P2P).

These weren't the most numerous files on the platforms, but there were still a *lot* of them. Grokster's catalog of non-infringing books and music was bigger than the entire collections of the biggest libraries and the entire stock of the biggest record stores. No one questioned that these were non-infringing, and it's hard to argue that a collection of works that's ranked among the world's largest isn't "substantial."

It's true that the founders of these P2P networks often blabbed to one another about how happy they were to see infringing works on their services, and included searches for top-forty music in their pitch-decks to investors and conference audiences. YouTube's founders crowed to one another about the unauthorized, infringing presence of popular works on the service, and schemed—in writing!—about how to get more of the same.

But remember: Sony *advertised* infringing uses for the Betamax. The company used copyright infringement as part of its sales pitch—and nevertheless, the Supreme Court in 1984 decided that VCRs were legit because of their "substantial non-infringing uses."

But the Supreme Court in 1984 cared a lot about its legitimacy. The 2005 court that ruled against Grokster—a decentralized successor to Napster—cared less. It neutered the "substantial non-infringing use" principle of *Betamax* and said that Grokster's "inducement" of infringement made it illegal, irrespective of the non-infringing uses it permitted.

That was the end of Grokster, and it was the end of raising VC money for file-sharing services. But it wasn't the end of copyright infringement. Starved of capital, file sharing went underground, turning to BitTorrent to distribute more files than ever. The

BitTorrent trackers that indexed the files on offer supported themselves with ads, moved their servers offshore, and thumbed their noses at the outraged legal demands of the entertainment industry's fiercest lawyers.

The *Grokster* case ended any hope of legitimizing file sharing. If you wanted to offer a music service, you had to cut a deal with the labels, and that deal would be limited to the songs that the labels were willing to permit. Gone were the bootlegs, live recordings and rarities that made P2P such a fannish delight. Instead, we got services like Pandora and Spotify, which offered a sanitized subset of the P2P catalog and raised investment capital from the labels themselves, functioning as semi-autonomous product development shops for the labels, separated by enough arms-length distance from meddling, conflicted record execs that they could finally develop a decent, popular service.

But Pandora and Spotify weren't public communications platforms. Users couldn't upload their own tracks or even annotations to the service. You could make a great playlist, but you couldn't chat with the author of that perfect playlist you just discovered. Spotify and Pandora were platforms where record labels could make works available to listeners, but they weren't places where listeners could participate.

Those person-to-person platforms became social media: YouTube, Facebook and Twitter. There's plenty wrong with these platforms, but from the media industry's perspective, their biggest problem was enabling members of the public to upload audio-visual works where other members of the public could get them.

This is a classic "substantial non-infringing use": the vast majority of texts, images, videos and sounds that members of the public put on social media are original to them (such as selfies, or 280-character thoughts, or cute animal videos, or ...) but these services are of unimaginable scale, and so even the minority of copyright infringing works that they host constitutes a vast pirate library.

These services are all *Betamax*'s progeny: they were all founded on the assumption that a product with substantial non-infringing uses would be safe from legal jeopardy. That assumption was backstopped by the 1998 Digital Millennium Copyright Act

(DMCA), whose Section 512—the "safe harbor"—says that online companies aren't liable for their users' copyright infringements, provided that they "expeditiously" remove their users' materials after receiving a complaint.

This "notice-and-takedown" system is meant to find a middle ground. It doesn't exactly treat an online service like a bookstore or a movie theater (which would face copyright liability if one of the works it offered to the public was found to infringe copyright).

Nor does it treat online services like a technology, say, Sony's Betamax. Even if you told Sony that it had a customer who used a Betamax to infringe copyright, Sony wouldn't be a party to the infringement and would have no obligation to stop selling VCRs to that customer.

It also doesn't treat online services like a private speech forum—like a bar or a restaurant, which has no obligation to monitor its customers' conversations for copyright infringement or act to prevent them.

Instead, notice-and-takedown borrows a little from all of these, saying to online companies: "You may assist members of the public in communicating with one another, and you have no duty to spy on their communications. If their communications are found to be infringing, you will not be liable, provided that you didn't ignore a takedown notice. You *can* ignore a takedown notice if you think it's bogus, but if you do, you might end up in court as a co-defendant with your user."

Notice-and-takedown has its problems. It's a rare company that subjects infringement notices to even cursory scrutiny, and this means that bad actors can have virtually anything removed from the internet by writing to the company that hosts it (or the company that hosts that company, or the company that provides its domain name service, or the company that provides its ads, or ...) and claiming to hold the copyright to whatever you want deleted. Most times, that will result in the material disappearing, whether or not you created it or have any claim over its copyright.

Theoretically, the notice-and-takedown system allows for "counternotices" from users who are targeted this way, but companies are free to ignore their protestations of innocence.

Notice-and-takedown is ripe for abuse, and many bad actors

have exploited its defects. For example, "reputation management" services working for dictators, rapists and organized crime figures routinely install blog software on their servers and then copy posts that criticize their clients, backdating the posts so that they appear to have been published long before the original posts. Then they send copyright notices to Google and other search tools, claiming that the original is an unauthorized copy (of their own unauthorized copy!) and demand that the original be removed from Google's search index. Then they either delete their copy, or alter it so that it praises, rather than condemns, their awful clients.

So if you're an awful boss who got fired for sexually harassing your employees, this company will copy your victims' tell-all posts to a WordPress blog and backdate them so they appear to be older than your victims' accounts. Then they'll write to Google and have your victims' posts removed from Google's search index, so anyone who searches your name won't see their posts; instead, they'll get links to posts controlled by the reputation management company.

That's pretty terrible, but if you posit an entertainment industry led by people with sociopathic disregard for the ways in which the laws that benefit themselves harm others, then perhaps this will strike you as acceptable collateral damage. Record and TV and movie execs aren't in the business of preventing criminals from laundering their reputations—they just want to reduce copyright infringement. If a rapey boss gets away with his crimes without suffering enduring reputational damage, that's someone else's problem, right?

Not even I am that cynical. Maybe there's an entertainment industry exec who's so depraved in their quest for regulatory dominance that they're thinking that way, but I suspect a majority of them are quietly horrified by this kind of thing.

But even if they're not, notice-and-takedown's vulnerabilities are also a real danger to creators and their ability to earn a living and disseminate their work. Creators have faced censorship at the hands of unsophisticated internet trolls who have mastered the trick of falsely claiming that your art offends their copyright, which is often sufficient to get the material removed.

This gets even worse where platforms go beyond the duties imposed by notice-and-takedown to create "three strikes" systems. YouTube is the most prominent three-strikes system: if your account attracts three copyright complaints, it is shuttered and all your work is deleted. That means you lose the ad revenue you got from your videos—and it means that you lose the Patreon revenue you get from using your videos to rope in paying subscribers. It means the loss of your work, and the loss of the search-engine mojo that brings new people to that work.

Triggering a third strike against a creator is devastating, and not everyone who defrauds YouTube into nuking an artist's account is doing it for the lulz; some of them are just running a business.

If you have mastered YouTube's arcane copyright system—a quasi-judicial system that can only be reliably operated by people who have diligently eked out the equivalent of a self-directed law degree in kangaroo court justice—you are in a tiny and privileged minority. It's a superpower, and the people who wield it are often supervillains.

Here's one supervillain scheme: find a YouTuber who's making a decent amount of money from their channel and file a couple of bogus copyright strikes against them. Then, privately message them and offer to remove those strikes on payment of a reasonable ransom—while threatening to add a third and final strike if they don't pay up.

YouTube kicks these criminals out of its system … when they catch them.

Extortion-by-copyright-enforcement is a danger to independent creators, not big labels and studios and publishers. Large entertainment companies don't have to go through the same self-serve, largely automated Kafkaesque copyright system on YouTube. They can just pick up the phone and call someone senior at Google. Pulling a copyright-extortion scam on Sony Pictures or Universal Music or Penguin Random House is like mugging the director of the FBI. For a petty criminal, it's a career-limiting move. This kind of blackmail con is almost entirely directed at independent creators.

The harms from notice-and-takedown itself don't directly

affect the big entertainment companies. But in 2007, the entertainment industry itself engineered a new, more potent form of notice-and-takedown that manages to inflict direct harm on Big Content, while amplifying the harms to the rest of us.

That new system is "notice-and-stay-down," a successor to notice-and-takedown that monitors everything every user uploads or types and checks to see whether it is similar to something that has been flagged as a copyrighted work. This has long been a legal goal of the entertainment industry, and in 2019 it became a feature of EU law, but back in 2007, notice-and-stay-down made its debut as a voluntary modification to YouTube, called "Content ID."

Some background: in 2007, Viacom (part of CBS) filed a billion-dollar copyright suit against YouTube, alleging that the company had encouraged its users to infringe on its programs by uploading them to YouTube. Google—which acquired YouTube in 2006—defended itself by invoking the principles behind *Betamax* and notice-and-takedown, arguing that it had lived up to its legal obligations and that *Betamax* established that "inducement" to copyright infringement didn't create liability for tech companies (recall that Sony had advertised the VCR as a means of violating copyright law by recording Hollywood movies and watching them at your friends' houses, and the Supreme Court decided it didn't matter).

But with *Grokster* hanging over Google's head, there was reason to believe that this defense might not fly. There was a real possibility that Viacom could sue YouTube out of existence—indeed, profanity-laced internal communications from Viacom —which Google extracted through the legal discovery process—showed that Viacom execs had been hotly debating which one of them would add YouTube to their private empire when Google was forced to sell YouTube to the company.

Google squeaked out a victory, but was determined not to end up in a mess like the Viacom suit again. It created Content ID, an "audio fingerprinting" tool that was pitched as a way for rightsholders to block, or monetize, the use of their copyrighted works by third parties. YouTube allowed large (at first) rightsholders to upload their catalogs to a blocklist, and then scanned all user uploads to check whether any of their audio matched a "claimed" clip.

Once Content ID determined that a user was attempting to post a copyrighted work without permission from its rightsholder, it consulted a database to determine the rightsholder's preference. Some rightsholders blocked any uploads containing audio that matched theirs; others opted to take the ad revenue generated by that video.

There are lots of problems with this. Notably, there's the inability of Content ID to determine whether a third party's use of someone else's copyright constitutes "fair use." As discussed, fair use is the suite of uses that are permitted even if the rightsholder objects, such as taking excerpts for critical or transformational purposes. Fair use is a "fact intensive" doctrine—that is, the answer to "Is this fair use?" is almost always "It depends, let's ask a judge."

Computers *can't* sort fair use from infringement. There is no way they ever can. That means that filters block all kinds of legitimate creative work and other expressive speech—especially work that makes use of samples or quotations.

But it's not just creative borrowing, remixing and transformation that filters struggle with. A lot of creative work is similar to *other* creative work. For example, a six-note phrase from Katy Perry's 2013 song "Dark Horse" is effectively identical to a six-note phrase in "Joyful Noise," a 2008 song by a much less well-known Christian rapper called Flame. Flame and Perry went several rounds in the courts, with Flame accusing Perry of violating his copyright. Perry eventually prevailed, which is good news for her.

But YouTube's filters struggle to distinguish Perry's six-note phrase from Flame's (as do the executives at Warner Chappell, Perry's publisher, who have periodically accused people who post snippets of Flame's "Joyful Noise" of infringing on Perry's "Dark Horse"). Even when the similarity isn't as pronounced as in Dark, Joyful, Noisy Horse, filters routinely hallucinate copyright infringements where none exist—and this is by design.

To understand why, first we have to think about filters as a security measure—that is, as a measure taken by one group of people (platforms and rightsholder groups) who want to stop another group of people (uploaders) from doing something they want to do (upload infringing material).

It's pretty trivial to write a filter that blocks exact matches: the labels could upload losslessly encoded pristine digital masters of everything in their catalog, and any user who uploaded a track that was digitally or acoustically identical to that master would be blocked.

But it would be easy for an uploader to get around a filter like this: they could just compress the audio ever-so-slightly, below the threshold of human perception, and this new file would no longer match. Or they could cut a hundredth of a second off the beginning or end of the track, or omit a single bar from the bridge, or any of a million other modifications that listeners are unlikely to notice or complain about.

Filters don't operate on exact matches: instead, they employ "fuzzy" matching. They don't just block the things that rights-holders have told them to block—they block stuff that's *similar* to those things that rightsholders have claimed. This fuzziness can be adjusted: the system can be made more or less strict about what it considers to be a match.

Rightsholder groups want the matches to be as loose as possible, because somewhere out there, there might be someone who'd be happy with a very fuzzy, truncated version of a song, and they want to stop that person from getting the song for free.

The looser the matching, the more false positives. This is an especial problem for classical musicians: their performances of Bach, Beethoven and Mozart inevitably sound an awful lot like the recordings that Sony Music (the world's largest classical music label) has claimed in Content ID. As a result, it has become nearly impossible to earn a living off of online classical performance: your videos are either blocked, or the ad revenue they generate is shunted to Sony. Even *teaching* classical music performance has become a minefield, as painstakingly produced, free online lessons are blocked by Content ID or, if the label is feeling generous, the lessons are left online but the ad revenue they earn is shunted to a giant corporation, stealing the creative wages of a music teacher.

Notice-and-takedown law didn't give rightsholders the internet they wanted. What kind of internet was that? Well, though entertainment giants said all they wanted was an internet free from copyright infringement, their actions—and the candid memos released in the Viacom case—make it clear that blocking infringement is a pretext for an internet where the entertainment companies get to decide who can make a new technology and how it will function.

Twenty years ago, I participated in something called the Broadcast Protection Discussion Group (BPDG), organized by the Motion Picture Association of America's (MPAA) Content Protection Technical Working Group (CPTWG). The details of this group's charter are an eye-glazing alphabet soup of even more initialisms, and recounting the skullduggery that ensued would risk making cerebrospinal fluid dribble out of your nostrils and ears.

However, in the broadest strokes, the BPDG was an interindustry committee of tech and entertainment companies who were drafting a law that a corrupt US congressman had promised to pass if they all signed off. This law, the "Broadcast Flag," would give the movie studios a veto over the design of all future computers.

I was there on behalf of the Electronic Frontier Foundation; I had my first day on the job at the first meeting of the BPDG. My colleagues and I asked a lot of importunate questions about whether it was seemly or even legal for companies to conspire to structure the entire digital future based on the fears and greed of a handful of coked-up Hollyweird fat cats.

The entertainment executives bristled at this—studio execs are all shouters, and the volume went up significantly. One of the group's chairs took the floor to explain that the goal wasn't to control the future—it was to create a "polite marketplace," where companies divided up their turf and stuck to it. If you wanted to make something involving entertainment, you'd have to get the entertainment industry's permission.

That, in a nutshell, is the internet that Big Content wanted—a polite marketplace where no one surprised them by inventing something to help artists and/or audiences unless they cleared it with the cartel first.

Twenty years later, the European Union gave it to them. The EU Digital Single Market (DSM) Directive was the most contested legislation in EU history, mostly thanks to a controversial notice-and-stay-down rule. This rule—dubbed the "filternet" proposal—sent 150,000 Europeans into the streets in protest, and sparked the largest petition in EU history.

The plan to amend the Directive required a simple majority on a procedural vote. The majority failed by only five votes, and afterward, ten Members of the European Parliament said they'd been confused and pressed the wrong button (their votes were changed in the official record, but thanks to a bizarre quirk of EU procedure, the vote still carried, despite the final total showing that it lost by five votes).

Notice-and-stay-down was incredibly controversial in the EU, not least because automatic filtering is prohibited by the General Data Protection Regulation (GDPR), the EU's landmark privacy regulation.

In the runup to the vote on notice-and-stay-down, Axel Voss, the German politician who backed the rule, repeatedly insisted that there was some way for tech companies to prevent their users from reposting banned, copyrighted material without using an automated filter, but he refused to answer follow-up questions on how this might be accomplished.

Once the vote was done, Voss admitted that notice-and-stay-down would require automated filters. The issue has been mired in EU legal disputes and constitutional challenges ever since.

The internet the entertainment industry wants is pretty similar to the internet that authoritarian governments want. Even before 9/11 (but especially afterward), governments all over the world, including in the United States and the United Kingdom, saw that tech companies could be a force multiplier for their own spying and control.

In the 1990s, the Clinton administration fought the "crypto wars," attempting to prohibit civilians from accessing working encryption. Instead, they wanted a rule that required all tech firms to install backdoors in their tools, so law enforcement (and spies) could read all their users' communications.

These proposals have never gone away. In 2022, the UK

government spent £500,000 on an ad campaign to discredit Facebook's rollout of encryption for WhatsApp. As the Snowden revelations demonstrated, the goal here isn't to prevent crime, but rather, to structure the tech sector as an arm of government, unburdened by the accountability constraints that governments operate under.

Just as the goal of the Broadcast Flag wasn't to enforce copyright, but rather to create a "polite marketplace" where every new technology made life easier for Big Content, the goal of encryption bans is to make life easier for domestic spies.

Think of the "geofence warrants" that played such a starring role in the US January 6th Insurrection hearings: the tech companies use data from our phones to track our every move. This allows governments to travel through time and space, to pick a place and time and say, "Hand over the identities of everyone who was there." Though the most famous use of this power was in identifying participants in a failed coup, the most *common* use is tracking protesters at Black Lives Matter rallies.

The EU is alarmingly comfortable with co-opting Big Tech to serve as an arm of the state. 2018's Terror Regulation (TERREG) is a notice-and-stay-down rule for "terrorist" and "extremist" content—a rule that gives platforms mere hours to comply with takedown orders, and, thereafter, to filter everything their users post to block reposts.

TERREG (and its national equivalents, like Germany's Netzdg) has all the problems of copyright-based filters, but with far higher stakes. Algorithmic enforcement of "terrorist" content bans leads to the automated deletion of archives of human rights violations that NGOs and survivors have painstakingly assembled for use by future tribunals and prosecutions.

Deputizing tech companies to solve law enforcement problems on their platforms is bad because of all the ways it fails—but it's also bad when it *works*.

Take the global trend in passing laws forcing Facebook, Google and (to a lesser extent) Apple to pay "license fees" for the links their users post to news articles. These "link taxes" start from the flawed assumption that linking to news articles is "stealing content." It's not. Fair use (and its global counterparts, like fair dealing) is fine with posting a link to a news story and a brief excerpt. Indeed, the news publishers calling for link taxes routinely link to and quote one another's coverage as part of their own articles, without seeking permission or paying a license fee.

There's good reasons for that. First, "the news" is something that, by definition, is discussed. "News" that no one is talking about is actually not news, it's "a secret." Second, the news sometimes gets it wrong—makes factual errors or material omissions. Even good news entities do this (think of the *New York Times'* credulous reporting on the Weapons of Mass Destruction lie, which helped sell the twenty-year, disastrous global war on terror, killing millions and destabilizing an entire region). Without the right to quote—and thus critique—the news, we're at the mercy of fallible reporters and their fallible editors.

Quoting the news isn't stealing. But you know what is stealing? *Actual stealing.* That is, ripping off ad-revenue money that news publishers are owed by their ad-tech partners.

This is something Google and Facebook do all the time. The FTC and Texas attorney general's antitrust cases against the duopoly—which controls a majority of the world's online search and display advertising—have revealed a series of outright frauds, such as the Jedi Blue bid-rigging program in which Google and Facebook secretly agreed to accept lower bids for ads on the publishers' sites in order to maximize their own returns.

This isn't the kind of metaphorical rip-off that publishers reference when they complain about being quoted by Google or Facebook users—it's an actual theft. Facebook and Google owe them money, and they don't cough up. On top of that obvious rip-off, there is the subtler one—Facebook and Google leverage their dominance of the ad market to extract sky-high fees from publishers and advertisers.

There's two ways of looking at this problem.

Call the first way "The answer to the machine is the machine." This is the link tax approach. It observes that the tech companies have a lot of money thanks to their ability to rip off the news industry, and it orders them to give some of that money back—but doesn't order them to stop ripping off the publishers.

It can't do that—otherwise there would be no money to pay the link tax with.

Call the second way "Not one penny for tribute." This is the idea that we should make it impossible for tech companies to go on ripping off publishers, not that they should have to kick back some of their ill-gotten gains to those publishers who are able to bargain for the largest share of the link tax money, though these largest publishers are probably not the ones getting rooked the worst by tech.

Link taxes, notice-and-stay-down, terrorism filters, and all the other proposals to transform Big Tech companies into gentler, more socially responsible behemoths all start from the premise that Big Tech's bigness is off-limits to regulation.

After all, Big Tech can't pay link taxes without monopoly profits. Big Tech can't afford $100 million–plus Content ID filters without monopoly profits. Big Tech can't afford terrorism filters without monopoly profits. Big Tech can't afford to hire armies of moderators to chase harassers and scammers around on its platforms without monopoly profits.

Every time we deputize tech companies with government-like enforcement duties, we make it that much harder to cut them down to size (because they need to be big to fulfill those duties) and that much harder for smaller tech to offer better, more user-centric services (because small tech companies, startups, co-ops, nonprofits and individual tinkerers can't afford to comply with the regulations that force them to police their users' conduct).

Perfecting Big Tech is like installing a constitutional monarchy: rather than dethroning the autocratic leaders of our tech world, these "fix tech" advocates demand that they suffer themselves to be draped in golden chains, held loosely in the hands of an aristocracy of regulators who are drawn from the senior ranks of the tech firms themselves.

The problem with Mark Zuckerberg exercising total, unaccountable dominion over the digital lives of 3 billion people isn't merely that he is incredibly bad at that job. The real problem is *that job should not exist*. No one should hold that much power. We don't need a better Zuck. *We need to abolish Zuck.*

That's where interoperability comes in.

If we force Mark Zuckerberg—and the leaders of Apple, Google, Amazon, Microsoft, Salesforce and other tech giants—to blast openings into their walled gardens so new entities can connect to their services, we can drain their power.

Every time one of these companies screws you over—by censoring your speech, or by failing to block the speech of someone who's harassing you, or by cloning your product and selling it over yours, or by blocking you from reaching your subscribers —you can just *leave*, without incurring the sky-high switching costs they've worked so hard to build into the system.

The rest of this book is devoted to exactly how we'd make that work. But for now, I want to end this chapter by noting that interoperability is fundamentally incompatible with "the answer to the machine is the machine" approaches to fixing tech.

If we make sites responsible for filtering all copyright infringement, we can't also say that they can't have the final word on what content their users can post and see, or which content is recommended to those users. Same goes for detecting and blocking terrorist content and obscenity. If we tell platforms that they have a duty to block harassment, we can't also tell them that *other services'* users will be able to interact with the users they're hosting.

We have to pick one: either we cut tech companies down to size, or we hold them accountable for their users' actions.

We've tried making Big Tech into better tech for decades. That project has been an abject failure. To make tech better, we have to make it smaller—small enough that the bad ideas, carelessness and blind spots of individual tech leaders are their problems, not everyone else's. We need lots of tech, run by lots of different kinds of people and organizations, and we need to make it as close to costless as possible to switch from one to the other.

4

Interop: From Computer Science to the Real World

We've already seen how the inescapable interoperability of universal computers enabled gopher and the iWork suite, but that's just for starters. The technological world we inhabit today was profoundly shaped by the ability of newcomers to hack interoperable add-ons, plug-ins and features into the technologies that came before them.

Not just digital technologies, either! Take cable television. Cable was born in 1950, when a TV salesman named Robert Tarlton in Lansford, Pennsylvania, got a bunch of local TV stores to club together and finance a commercial "community antenna." This was a giant antenna, tall enough to pull in signals from Philadelphia, 90 miles away. The antenna was connected to TV owners' homes by means of a web of cables strung on poles.

The point was to goose the sales of TVs by expanding the range of channels local people could receive. Small, cooperative community antennas had been built before, but Tarlton's project was the first commercial, city-wide operation, and it was a smashing success, driving demand for new TVs.

This was not uncontroversial! The broadcasters whose signals Tarlton was commercially redistributing thought that he should have asked their permission, which, if they'd granted it, would have been contingent on a license fee for each customer.

CATV systems (as cable was known then) took off in towns across the USA, and with them came lawsuits. The whole matter was settled through a series of FCC actions that established that CATV operators didn't need permission to redistribute broadcast signals, but they *did* need to pay a set license fee. That is the arrangement US cable operators still rely on, and while broadcasters once bitterly decried the FCC for legalizing piracy, today, the license fees from cable are absolutely essential to broadcasters' operations. Broadcasters and cable operators often lobby as a single industry body, and both have joined forces against their common enemy, internet-based video services.

The rise and rise of cable TV is a fascinating tale of how interoperability can help an industry advance, even when it doesn't want to.

Remember that TV wasn't the original broadcast industry—long before the first commercial TV broadcast, there was a thriving commercial radio industry. Radio, too, was the beneficiary of interoperability.

When radio launched, it presented a competitive threat to the recorded music industry, and the largest and most powerful recording artists' organization, ASCAP, founded in 1914, was vehemently opposed to the playing of their records over the air. In 1941 it organized a boycott of radio, preventing the popular music of white, respectable musicians from reaching the airwaves.

But another musicians' group took a different tack—BMI (Broadcast Music Inc.). BMI represented "race music" and "hillbilly music" (Black music and country music) acts, these being two groups that ASCAP excluded from membership as being unfit for polite society. BMI embraced radio play, leaving ASCAP's artists fuming as America's airwaves became saturated with this "illegitimate" music while their own music was sidelined. ASCAP's members revolted, ended the boycott after ten months, and forced ASCAP to license their music for radio as well.

When TV came along, radio broadcasters adopted it as an adjunct to their existing services. It was these broadcast companies who insisted that cable should not exist without their permission and control—and never mind that they owed their own existence to their ability to launch a new medium without the consent of the recording artists, who dominated the previous wave of technological progress.

What's more, the record executives and recording artists who waged war on the radio were themselves the victors in yet another fight over technological disruption: sound recordings.

Before the rise of sound recording, the only music "industry" was sheet music production. Sheet music was an industry in that it involved an industrial process (printing) and a distribution system to get the products of that process into customers' hands.

Meanwhile, the actual musicians—the performers who turned printed sheets into music at halls and opera houses—were considered mere instruction-followers. The recipe for the music— the composition—was what mattered. Any competent crafts- person could use that recipe to produce the music that the skilled composer had originated.

But then phonograms came along, and these jumped-up recipe- followers started to record themselves performing the music, and to sell those recordings. As far as the composers and the sheet music industry were concerned, this was an act of sheer piracy, profiting off the labor of a composer without their permission.

John Philip Sousa, one of the most famous composers in America, railed against this before Congress in 1906, saying:

> When I was a boy ... in front of every house in the summer eve-
> nings you would find young people together singing the songs of
> the day or the old songs. Today you hear these infernal machines
> going night and day. We will not have a vocal cord left. The vocal
> cords will be eliminated by a process of evolution, as was the tail
> of man when he came from the ape.

Rather than banning the infernal machines, Congress legalized them at the stroke of a pen, creating a "compulsory license" that allowed anyone to re-record a cover of any song that had already been released and release it themselves, without the composer's permission, provided they paid a set royalty for every record.

The recording artists who enriched themselves by taking the songwriters' compositions without permission were the very same people who waged war on the radio for taking their records without permission. The broadcasters who waged war on the cable operators were the same companies who waxed fat by taking the recording artists' music without permission.

Congress stepped in to save cable, creating another blanket license: provided a cable operator pays a set rate per channel, it can suck in any broadcast programs its antenna can pick up and sell access to them over cable.

In 1976, it was the cable companies—who grew rich by taking broadcast signals without permission—who launched the *Betamax* suit, arguing that VCRs should be banned because they took cable signals without permission.

And Sony—the company that won the *Betamax* case and established that broadcast signals could be captured and re-used without permission—was one of the primary belligerents in the Napster wars and was a coplaintiff in the *Grokster* case, arguing that its media divisions (acquired after the *Betamax* case) were being abused by P2P companies who made products that interoperated with theirs without permission.

Without interoperability, there'd have been no radio or broadcast TV, no cable TV and no VCRs.

What's more, the interoperability that underpinned all of these revolutionary technological changes was a highly specific *kind* of interoperability: *adversarial* interoperability.

Though this book focuses on interoperability without permission —the kind of hard-fought interop that you get from reverse engineering a file format or network protocol and getting into protracted guerrilla warfare with some dominant, deep-pocketed company—there's an awful lot of *cooperative* interoperability out there.

Your house, your car, your appliances, your computer, even things like the paper in your books and the chemicals in your ink, are all designed to comply with *standards*. These are formal, technical documents that set out the allowable parameters for a product or service.

Standards are sometimes encoded in law (for example, the safety standards that keep your wall plugs from bursting into flames), and sometimes they're voluntary (like the AAA battery standard the company that made your TV remote used to ensure you could use any IEC R03 or ANSI C18.1 24 battery).

The IEC (International Electrotechnical Commission) and

ANSI (American National Standards Institute) are *standards bodies* or *standards development organizations*. These are (nominally) nonprofits that provide a forum and a set of institutional processes that allow "stakeholders" (companies, nonprofits, academics, government regulators and interested parties) to agree upon a set of technical specifications, such as the size, shape and power characteristics of an AAA battery.

Standards may be voluntary (as with your TV remote) or mandatory (as with your home plumbing, which is governed by your town's safety standards), but they are all *cooperative*. The whole point of making a standard battery is to ensure that it works with anyone's TV remote, and the point of designing a TV remote to work with AAA batteries is to ensure that any AAA battery will work with it.

Beyond *cooperative* interoperability, there is also *indifferent* interoperability. That's when someone makes a new product that plugs into an existing one that was not designed with the new product in mind, but which was *also* not designed to prevent this from happening.

Many gas stations have a fishbowl full of cheap car-lighter USB adapters next to the cash register. These "automobile auxiliary power outlets" are defined in ANSI/SAE J563, a standard jointly administered by ANSI and SAE, which used to be called the "Society of Automotive Engineers" until it grew to include standards for aerospace.

These were designed to hold push-button coil lighters that would transform 12V power into heat, allowing you to ignite a cigarette. Today, though, those twelve volts of available power are almost exclusively used to run chargers.

These chargers began as proprietary plugs for CB radios and GPS units, but gradually standardized on USB-A connectors (whose parameters are set by a standards body called the USB Implementers Forum).

When these chargers first appeared, their design and installation were not associated with the automakers. The design committees that created the cars the chargers went into never planned on accommodating chargers. The subcontractors who created the lighter sockets did not have chargers in mind.

But! When chargers *did* appear, the automakers and their subcontractors didn't fight them. They didn't try to block non-lighters from the lighter receptacle. There was no need to wage guerrilla warfare on the manufacturers.

Crucially, though, the manufacturers did not—at first—take steps to help you charge your gadgets with your lighter, either.

They were indifferent.

Indifferent interoperability is, if anything, even more common than cooperative interoperability. Nike won't stop you from using generic drug-store laces in your running shoes, but they won't help you, either. You can mix paint with your kitchen mixer, or use your screwdriver as a pry-tip. You can take a cool poster to any framer, who can mix-and-match any frame, matte and glass. Your toothbrush works with any toothpaste—and vice versa. Even "smart" toothbrushes! Your pillow takes any pillowcase. There are dozens of companies that will sell you plastic sleeves to protect your ridiculous, odd-sized CDC Covid proof-of-vaccination.

Without interoperability, our lives would be far more constrained, in good times and especially in bad times.

It's one thing to be stuck without the blender attachment that will make your smoothie perfectly smooth. But it's another thing for your blender to refuse to operate because it can't connect to its app because severe weather just knocked out your home internet and you're trying to mix your kid's medicine into a smoothie to get it down their throat.

That's something we learned a lot about from Covid, as lockdowns and disrupted supply chains exposed the brittleness created by manufacturers' war on interop.

Take Epson, the printer giant. Like most printer companies, Epson makes outsized profits by locking its customers into using its official ink, which is sold at prices that make vintage Champagne seem a bargain by comparison. Of course, Epson's customers would strongly prefer to pay less for ink, so Epson has to find some way to force them to pay through the nose.

To accomplish this, Epson embeds cheap microchips in its official ink cartridges, which are preloaded with secret cryptographic keys at the factory. When you put an ink cartridge in your

Epson printer, the printer generates a random number, a "nonce" —and yes, British readers, I fully appreciate how funny you find this cryptographer's term of art—and sends it to the chip on the cartridge.

That chip uses its cryptographic key to "sign" the nonce (generating a new number that combines the key and the random number, which is called "hashing") and sends the signature back to the printer. The printer also has a preloaded cryptographic key, which it can use to verify the signature. If the signature verifies, the cartridge is approved for use and the printer will send commands to it, allowing it to print.

The pandemic triggered mass shortages in microchips, especially cheap, low-powered chips used for applications like this one. It got so bad that some carmakers scoured warehouses for deadstock clothes washers that could be disassembled for their embedded controller chips, which could be repurposed to finish cars that came off the line minus their microchips.

This was a problem for Epson: its printers were designed to block any ink cartridge unless it had an official Epson-configured chip—and it couldn't get the chips! In the end, Epson started selling chipless cartridges, along with *instructions for bypassing its own security chips*.

It's hard to express just how weird and perverse this is: Epson is part of the coalition of companies that have waged technological and legal warfare upon anyone who dared challenge their anti-interoperability products. Now here the company was, telling anyone with an internet connection how to disable those anti-interop "features," making it easy for Epson printer owners to use ink of their choosing.

I admit a grudging respect for Epson, which chose its customers' ability to use their printers during a global pandemic over its shareholders' ability to collect 10,000 percent margins on its ink.

Especially since not every company made the same call.

Medtronic is the largest med-tech company in the world, thanks to a string of anticompetitive mergers that let it gobble up most of its competitors. The company is also responsible for the largest-ever "tax inversion," a financial maneuver in which Medtronic "sold itself" to a much smaller Irish company.

Ireland is one of the EU's most notorious onshore tax havens, and Medtronic's reverse takeover let it claim that all its profits were suspended in a state of tax-free grace somewhere over the Irish Sea.

Medtronic makes the workhorse PB840 ventilator, which is to be found in hospitals all over the world. Now, hospitals are accustomed to fixing their own equipment—for obvious reasons. When a key piece of medical equipment breaks down, you call for the on-site engineer to come and fix it, because waiting hours or days for the manufacturer's rep to show up and do the repair can be a matter of life or death for your patients.

But repair is a potential source of windfall profits for manufacturers. If manufacturers can force their customers to turn exclusively to them for service, then the manufacturer can require that all repairs involve new, original parts—no refurbs or third-party spares. Freed from competition, manufacturers can charge arbitrary sums for repair. Best of all: manufacturers get to decide when your gadget is beyond repair, and they can send that gizmo to a landfill and sell you a new one.

The war on repair has many fronts: cars and iPhones, tractors and electric shavers. Medtronic brought the war to ventilators.

Like inkjet cartridges, key assemblies in the PB840 contain a cheap microchip that ships with a factory-supplied cryptographic key. When a part is installed in a PB840, the PB840's central control unit cryptographic challenges the new part in much the same way that an inkjet printer challenges a new cartridge. If the challenge fails, the ventilator refuses to work with it.

This process is called VIN-locking, a term from the automotive industry (VIN stands for "Vehicle Identification Number," the unique serial number that is engraved on each car's chassis and embedded in its computer control unit at the factory).

VIN-locked devices don't just validate that all of their parts come from the original manufacturer, they also ensure that these parts were *installed by the manufacturer's official technicians.* Before a VIN-locked component can be used by a device, an authorized technician has to enter an unlock code so the device knows that new part was installed by someone who charged for it and passed the payment on to the company and its shareholders.

This means that when a farmer's John Deere tractor breaks and they swap in a working part, the tractor remains immobilized until one of Deere's technicians shows up at the end of the lonely country road to give the repair a once-over and type in an access code.

John Deere tractors are among the most notorious users of VIN-locking. The company—a monopolist that bought out nearly every other tractor company, until most of our global food supply was dependent on its products—has been a world leader in the fight against the "right to repair."

Deere says that farmers are basically yokels who can't be trusted with the newfangled, computerized wonders that the company delivers to them. The fact that John Deere gets to bill farmers a couple hundred dollars every time its tractors break down is, according to Deere, just an incredible coincidence.

Like hospitals, farms are the site of time-sensitive technology usage. When your patient needs a ventilator, you can't afford to wait for Medtronic to send out a technician to approve your repair. When the hailstorm is coming and you need to bring the crops in, you can't afford to wait for Deere to run its tawdry $200 repair racket.

That's why farms have had their own workshops since the dawn of agriculture. Ancient Roman farmhouses have attached workshops with their own forges. Farmers—geographically isolated and faced with an ever-shifting array of idiosyncratic challenges—have always repaired and improved on their tools.

That includes their tractors.

For years, the John Deere company dispatched field engineers to tour the farms where its tractors were in use, making note of the modifications and improvements that farmers had made, incorporating them into future models of their tractors.

This meant that John Deere's ability to sell upgrades, parts, attachments and repairs was always contingent on the company's ability to make better products and offer better services than the local mechanic or one of hundreds of small firms that made specialized add-ons.

But the combination of digitization and lax antitrust changed that. Digitization meant that Deere could VIN-lock its tractors, using ever-cheaper embedded microcontrollers to check for a digital handshake between each part and add-on. Meanwhile, lax antitrust meant that Deere could trumpet this capability to the capital markets, which showered the company in cash that it used to buy out all its rivals, so that VIN-locked tractors came to dominate global agriculture.

VIN-locking is proliferating at a terrifying pace. US users of powered wheelchairs routinely find themselves stranded because their chairs are VIN-locked and can't be serviced by a local repair shop; even minor changes like adjusting motor torque to take account of new tires require an appointment with an official service technician. There are VIN locks in medical implants and in smart home tech—you've got them inside your body, and you put your body inside them.

Bypassing VIN locks and other forms of restrictive technology is often technologically simple. Universal computers can run any program, and VIN locks run on universal computers, so one need merely write a program that can neutralize the lock and then proceed with your own ink, ventilator screens, tractor parts, wheelchair settings or other adjustments.

Those who would defeat these locks have the "attacker's advantage." For a system like a VIN lock to work, its authors must write code with no errors. For the system to be defeated, their adversaries need only find a single error and exploit it. Defenders need to be perfect, while attackers do not.

That's not to say that anyone can defeat a VIN lock or other anti-user technology. You need real technical expertise to do this, to be sure, but once you've done it—once you've reverse engineered the technology and found and exploited a flaw in it —you can embody that exploit in a program, which anyone can run.

This is a marvelous and underappreciated facet of software. Code is often compared to a recipe, but speaking as someone who has diligently followed numerous recipes with disappointing results, I am here to tell you that simply because someone has provided you with detailed instructions for accomplishing some difficult task, it doesn't follow that you can actually perform that task.

But code is different. Every day, in millions of ways, I perform tasks I am completely incompetent to accomplish, simply by clicking some buttons or typing some commands into my computer. This invokes software, which then self-executes. If code is a recipe, it's a recipe for a meal that cooks itself. Every program is a little robot, imbued by its programmers with a sliver of their expertise, which it will turn into an action, on demand, endlessly.

So if you happen to have the skill to locate an imperfection in the digital lock code restricting some piece of technology, and to drive a wedge into that crack and split the lock wide open, and if you turn that into a program, a self-executing recipe, then even mediocrities like me can wield it. You can catch some of your skill and power in a few lines of code and distribute it to the ends of the Earth, and anyone who runs that code can briefly channel all your insight and experience and skill in order to break the locks that bind them.

The designers of digital locks appreciate this fact. Publicly, they'll insist that their locks are strong enough to stop all comers. But their actions speak louder than their words.

You see, digital locks have a unique position in the global legal system. In the mid-1990s, a pair of UN treaties—the WIPO Copyright Treaty and the WIPO Performers and Phonograms Treaty—created a new, worldwide legal regime for these locks.

These treaties (they're colloquially called "the Internet Treaties") bind UN member states to establish special protections for digital locks. The USA established its version of these protections in 1998, with the passage of the Digital Millennium Copyright Act (DMCA). Section 1201 of the DMCA makes it a felony, punishable by a five-year prison sentence and a $500,000 fine, to "traffic" in a tool that can bypass "an effective means of access control." The law is so broadly written that merely publishing information that could help someone beat an "access control" is a crime.

Now, if digital locks worked on their own, the DMCA would be superfluous. The reason you can't read someone else's encrypted email is that it's technologically impossible, not because it's illegal—just as the reason burglars can't scale the barbed-wire fence around a junkyard is that they'll cut their hands to ribbons, not because burglary is a crime. Barbed-wire fences work the same whether or not burglary is illegal.

That's not true of digital locks. Any sufficiently skilled security practitioner can defeat any digital lock, and because this all transpires in the realm of software, that practitioner can encapsulate and share their expertise with all comers, merely by writing a program that automates their findings.

The digital locks that prevent technology users from taking control over the products and services they use—that prevent us from loading non–Apple-approved software on an iPhone, or from using a non–Facebook-approved program to communicate with our friends stuck inside Facebook's walled garden—are very poor *technical* defenses.

Indeed, the point of these locks is not to stand up to outsiders and prevent them from doing things that are adverse to the interests of Big Tech shareholders. Rather, the point of adding a lock to a product is to *gain the right to invoke Section 1201 of the DMCA.*

Once the software that powers a product has been wrapped in the thinnest skin of digital locks, then any competitor who wants to alter how that software works—say, to enable you to use third-party ink in your printer or third-party batteries in your phone—has to remove the digital lock.

Section 1201 of the DMCA felonizes removing a digital lock. Thus, the presence of a digital lock constitutes a countermeasure whose *legal* force is far more powerful than its *technical* force. Even if you can figure out how to break a digital lock, telling anyone how you did it, or making a tool so they can do it too, becomes a felony.

This represents a seismic shift in our relationship to the products and services we buy. Historically, buying something made it yours to use as you saw fit. If your microwave oven was sold at a discount because it was a low-end model whose turntable was immobilized, you could go out and buy a third-party turntable at Wal-Mart, and the manufacturer didn't get to stop you.

The manufacturer's plan to segment its market by limiting the capabilities of its low-end offerings was its business, not yours. You were under no obligation to respect the manufacturer's business model. They sold you the product, you bought it, end of story. If the manufacturer didn't like how you used the product, it could go fuck itself.

But Section 1201 of the DMCA forces you to respect the shareholders' priorities, even when they conflict with your own —or else.

In the decades since the DMCA's passage, the cost of micro-controllers has undergone an absolutely foreseeable plummet. Today, chips are so cheap as to be effectively free (notwithstanding the pandemic-related, transient supply-chain shock). That fact, combined with the rules against breaking a digital lock, has profoundly shifted the calculus for product designers.

Today, the US government's offer to product makers is: "If you add a chip to your gadget at a price of a mere $0.26, and load a digital lock onto that chip that nominally prevents a customer from using the product in a way you don't like, we, the mighty US government, will lend you our courts, our federal prosecutors, and our prisons so you can terrorize anyone who provides your customer with a lock-removing tool. It does not matter if anyone's copyright is violated. It does not matter if *any* right is violated. The mere act of providing a tool to remove the lock—no matter how benign and beneficial the purpose—triggers criminal and civil liability for your commercial rivals."

This offer is very tempting. Digital locks are in wheelchairs, insulin pumps, coffee makers, car engines, toaster ovens, tractors, lightbulbs, phones, ventilators, McDonald's soft-serve ice-cream machines, sex toys and more devices every day. Digital locks are proliferating *within* devices, as well, providing for finer-grained corporate control—for example, Apple's iPhone screens and batteries have VIN locks that can distinguish between an official repair and a third-party repair.

This should surprise no one. Section 1201 of the DMCA is a pure moral hazard. What corporate executive would pass up an offer from Uncle Sam that went, "We will make it a felony to thwart your commercial ambitions?" As Jay Freeman—who created Cydia, an independent app store for iPhones—says, any manufacturer who includes a digital lock gets to prosecute their rivals for felony contempt of business model.

Every one of these giant corporations has a building full of lawyers next to a building full of engineers. Though they style themselves as tech companies, they don't act like it. If a rival has the temerity to make use of adversarial interoperability to unlock the restrictions on their products, the company's executives don't call on their engineers to beef up the locks and kick the intruders out of the gadgets they make. They go straight to their lawyers, demanding action under Section 1201 of the DMCA.

Now, I'm fully aware that non-Americans reading this might be feeling a little smug. *Oh, those foolish Americans, so in thrall to corporate lobbyists! What foolish laws they have brought into their law books!*

Not so fast.

The DMCA came to the USA through the WIPO Internet Treaties. WIPO—the World Intellectual Property Organization—is a "specialized agency" of the United Nations. Originally founded as an international lobbying organization for big business, WIPO was folded into the UN in 1974.

The Internet Treaties have a weird history. In the early 1990s, Al Gore—then vice president to Bill Clinton—convened a series of hearings on the demilitarization and commercialization of the internet. These were called the "National Information Infrastructure" hearings, or, more colloquially, the "Information Superhighway" hearings.

All kinds of people showed up at Gore's hearings and sent in their wild—and sometimes harebrained—schemes for producing an "information superhighway," but the cake was taken by a sublime weirdo named Bruce Lehman.

Bill Clinton hired Lehman away from Microsoft to serve as his "IP czar." Microsoft had responded to the internet with a series of doomed bids to kill it and replace it with a network of Microsoft's design, under Microsoft's control. These were laughably terrible and roundly despised, but Microsoft had a secret weapon: a monopoly. After repeatedly failing to launch its own competitor to the internet, Microsoft poured its energies into promoting its terrible browser, Internet Explorer (colloquially called "Internet Exploder" due to its propensity to crash at the least provocation) by redesigning Windows so that other browsers (notably Netscape Navigator) couldn't run properly. This was so egregious—and made so many rich people angry—that the DoJ eventually brought an antitrust suit against Microsoft, dragging up old memories of the "DOS isn't done until Lotus won't run" days. Seven years later, Microsoft was convicted, but it appealed and wriggled free. More on this later.

Lehman had presided over much of this conduct while at Microsoft, and he was a true partisan for Bill Gates's vision of "intellectual property," grounded in the idea that every intangible thing should be made scarce through systems of control, the rents from which would promote investment and innovation.

As Copyright Czar, Lehman delivered his vision of the Information Superhighway to Gore, and it was truly something. Lehman envisioned a system of copyright permissions that could have been mistaken for satire, calling for negotiated license deals for every copy of a work, even within a computer or across a network. This would have provided full employment for every copyright lawyer alive and yet to be born, but it would have made for a seriously broken internet.

Gore, to his everlasting credit, dismissed Lehman out of hand. But Lehman was undaunted. He wrangled a new post as the US Trade Representative delegate to WIPO, then flew to Geneva and turned his laughably terrible ideas into the Internet Treaties.

The Digital Millennium Copyright Act is the US's implementation of the Internet Treaties. It's a law that was rejected by elected American officials when it was proposed by a former executive from the century's most notorious monopolist. So that same unelected revolving-door-rider caught a flight to Switzerland and got the UN to *order* the Americans to pass his law, which they dutifully did. That's how the sausage gets made.

The US Trade Representative has spent the past two decades scurrying around the world, arm-twisting America's trade partners into coming into compliance with the Internet Treaties. That means that laws that are functionally identical to the DMCA are on the books in practically every country on Earth.

The EU adopted them in 2001, with Article 6 of the EU Copyright Directive. Canada got its version in 2012, with the passage of Bill C-11. As a Canadian, I find this genuinely embarrassing;

American lawmakers have a credible argument that when they passed the DMCA in 1998, it wasn't obvious that it would have far-reaching, negative effects as computers permeated more kinds of devices and components—but the Canadian MPs who voted for C-11 in 2012 have no such excuse. Instead, they had the benefit of fourteen years' worth of DMCA debacles to draw on.

Other countries came onboard piecemeal. Russia signed on to DMCA-like rules when it joined the World Trade Organization. The WTO agreement includes the TRIPS Agreement (TRIPS is an acronym for Trade-Related Aspects of Intellectual Property Rights), which includes the Internet Treaties. All WTO members have an obligation to adopt the DMCA's prohibition on breaking digital locks.

The Andean nations of South America fell into line through a series of trade deals with the United States, while Central American countries were brought onboard through the Central American Free Trade Agreement (CAFTA).

Mexico was a latecomer to the party, adopting a particularly dreadful version of these rules in 2020, during the Covid lockdowns, without any substantive debate. The ensuing outrage prompted the Mexican Supreme Court to take up the question of whether the law passed Mexican Constitutional muster.

The point being: wherever you live, your government has probably adopted "anti-circumvention" rules protecting digital locks, with far-reaching legislation or regulation that bans breaking these locks for any purpose, even perfectly legal ones.

Yes, America got there first, and yes, America arm-twisted the rest of the world into adopting these rules, but this is not an American issue, because they succeeded, and so everywhere you go, you'll find rules that block interoperability.

From the perspective of a company hoping to block interop—and maintain the high switching costs that hold their users hostage—Section 1201 of the DMCA is a powerful tool, far better than any technical tool that the companies have at their disposal.

If a company uses its building full of engineers to fight interoperators, it takes on all kinds of costs and risks. The engineers who are busy doing battle with the guerrilla fighters seeking to connect to their systems aren't able to contribute to the products that actually make money for the firm. The attacker's advantage means that the would-be interoperators are fighting on the right side of an asymmetric war, where it takes less effort to connect to the service than it costs to block connections.

What's more, the engineers who are tasked with defending their service are harder to replace than lawyers who might wield the DMCA to exclude those rivals: any competent lawyer can brief a judge, but engineers familiar with the inner workings of Big Tech's systems and services are specialized and rare.

Worse: even if the big company's engineers manage to repel the invaders, that does nothing to stop the next wave of would-be interoperators from challenging them anew.

Contrast this with a DMCA-based legal strategy: if a corporate exec passes over the building full of lawyers and heads instead to the building full of engineers, the best they can hope for is that their engineers—scarce and needed to create and maintain the company's products—will beat back some sharp-elbowed interoperator, overpowering an adversary who has the much easier task of attacking while you play defense. That victory, if it comes, is a one-off. The next interoperator who comes along can kick off a fresh, endless round of hand-to-hand asymmetric warfare.

But if the exec passes over the building full of engineers and goes straight to the lawyers, there is the prospect of immediate and enduring total victory. The lawyer can get an injunction to block the interoperator, forcing them to halt immediately. They can file a suit against the interoperator, seeking sky-high damages and, in the case of a DMCA 1201 claim, criminal sanctions.

Just the process of going to court is a victory of sorts, here. Every other technologist who contemplates a similar interoperability project will be intimidated by the prospect of facing the same treatment. The investors who backed the original interoperator will learn that you can't win a bet against Big Tech, as will the investors' competitors, who will get the same message and forebear from funding such endeavors, likely forever.

Any customers the interoperator had—say, Apple iPhone owners who invested in buying apps from a rival, interoperable app store—will learn that this kind of interoperability-based business is built on unsound foundations, and steer clear of similar enterprises in future.

In other words, a legal victory is *far* more devastating than a mere technical one. A firm that sues a rival into oblivion for aiding its customers in grabbing a better experience for themselves (better prices, more privacy or just a user interface that's better adapted to their capabilities and disabilities) wins a powerful prize.

That firm can use the law to reach beyond its four walls, into the minds of potential future competitors and their investors, and permanently terrorize them out of even the merest thought of a challenge to the company's dominance. That firm can reach into the hearts of its own customers and convince them that any attempt to disloyally reconfigure their experience of the firm's products will be a futile waste of hope.

Venture capitalists call the products and services adjacent to the Big Tech firms' core technology "the kill zone" and will not invest in any company that proposes to pitch its tent in that dead place.

Abandon all hope, ye who enter here.

5

Standards and Mandates: What's Behind the Shield of Boringness?

So, let's force them to interoperate.

That's what laws like the ACCESS Act (US) and Digital Markets Act (EU) propose to do: they propose technology "mandates" that force the largest tech companies to provide a reliable, standardized "interface" to their systems for interoperators to use.

For example, Facebook (which, bizarrely, insists that it is called "Meta") would have to provide a standard way for members of other online communities to send and receive private messages with its users, and access the group discussions taking place on Facebook.

These rival social media companies would connect to a server on Facebook and exchange structured messages on behalf of their users, sending and receiving personal notes and posts for public and private groups.

Obviously, this raises some privacy issues: what if you think you're sending a private message to a Facebook friend who's departed for a rival service, but it's actually an impersonator? Or what if the rival service decides to make that private message public? What if it's run by a foreign state adversary, looking to steal your identity so they can break into your company servers? What if it's run by criminals looking to trick you into installing malicious software on your computer?

Both the ACCESS Act and the DMA take different approaches to answering these questions, which we'll dig into later. But for now, I want to get into a different kind of issue, one that might not be so obvious unless you've spent a lot of time working in a very specialized subfield of technology: standardization.

"Standards" are a catch-all term for the precise technical specifications that allow multiple products or components to work together. The ANSI/SAE J563 standard for your car's cigarette lighter is one such standard: it defines the physical shape of a receptacle (so that you'll know that any plugs you buy for it will fit) as well as the maximum and minimum voltage and amperage it supplies (so that it will actually power your devices but not damage either them or your car's electrical subsystem). It also defines some safety features that *should* make it fail gracefully in the event of a short or some other unexpected event (rather than, say, melting down).

Standards are all around you: the wall receptacle you plug your appliances and chargers into is a standard size; has standard plugs; delivers a standard current; connects to a wire that passes through a conduit of standard materials; strength and flexibility; and finally terminating in your breaker panel, where standardized breakers condition and distribute power from standardized utility mains coming out of a subterranean utility conduit or off a pole beside your home.

That's a lot of standards, and it's only scratching the surface. The processes for refining the copper in the wires and the aluminum in the receptacle are standardized; so are the ways your utility measures your power consumption. The paper your bill comes on is standardized (likely US Letter in the United States and Canada, and A4 in the rest of the world) and it fits in a standard envelope. Those standards are how anyone can design a printer that can correctly print a bill and address an envelope.

It's fashionable today to talk about "infrastructure"—the systems and objects that make life possible. Normally we talk about roads and water delivery and sewers as infrastructure, or power plants and even data centers, but standards are also infrastructure, and indeed, they are infrastructure *for* infrastructure. It's foolish to try to build a road without standards—what if it's too narrow for vehicle traffic?

Infrastructure choices cast a long shadow. Take roads: the

width of the Roman roads was the width of the wheelbase of Roman chariots, itself a function of the state of the art of Roman metallurgy, which determined the maximum length of a stable axle.

The chariot roads became cart roads, and the cart roads became motor-vehicle roads. Long after we had the ability to extend the wheelbase of a motor vehicle beyond the limits of Roman metal-beating, we were locked into roads that could be served by the blacksmiths of the Classical Age.

The width of the road determined the width of a train container because of intermodal transport, where freight containers are moved from flat railcars to flatbed trucks. Any efficiencies that could be realized by making freight containers wider than what a flatbed truck could handle would be erased by the extra work of unloading that container's contents and repacking it into one that was road-sized.

So it was that the track clearances along the rights-of-way for railroads were sized to accommodate a freight car, with a little space on either side. Shipping anything wider than a freight car became a complex business, requiring advance scouting along the whole route to make sure the cargo wouldn't clip a tree branch, utility pole or building.

The design for the Space Shuttle called for the creation of reusable solid rocket boosters, massive cone-tipped cylinders that would lift the Shuttle to 150,000 feet before falling away and floating to the ground on parachutes for recovery and reuse. This worked surprisingly well.

The boosters were built in Box County, Utah, and shipped to Florida for takeoff. After each use, they'd be recovered from the open ocean, freighted to port, refurbished and, once again, shipped to Florida.

The boosters were about 150 feet long, but they were precisely 12.17 feet in diameter—because they had to fit on a special railway flatcar for those overland shipments.

The aerospace engineers who sat down to design those solid rocket boosters had a lot of parameters to juggle—the pull of gravity, the efficiency of rocket fuel, the weight of the payload. But mixed in with those parameters, immutable and inarguable was the width of a railcar, which was foreordained by the width of the Roman chariot wheelbase, which was, in turn, determined by the metalbeating know-how of Roman blacksmiths.

Infrastructure casts a long shadow.

Standards are infrastructure. Infrastructure casts a long shadow. A company that can bend standards to preference its products, its patents or its capabilities can lock in an enduring advantage.

In an ideal world, standards would be a kind of cool scientific enterprise, carefully conceived to ensure that our informational infrastructure was sturdy, flexible and powerful. The ideal standardization process would anticipate the efforts of corporations and cartels to preference their technologies and take steps to make sure the process was fair.

However, standards organizations are generally optimized *for* corporate capture. Standards bodies' funding comes from a mix of dues (sometimes with larger companies paying higher dues) and selling access to the finished standards once they're published.

Even though they are typically structured as nonprofits, many standards bodies pay their top executives salaries in the millions (the fact that they *are* nonprofits means they have to publish this data; the CEOs of Underwriters' Laboratories, the National Sanitation Foundation, and the British Standards Institution all take home more than one million dollars in salary every year). Beyond sky-high executive compensation, standards bodies employ administrators, legal counsel, house technologists and a slew of other personnel.

The job of those employed by a standards body is to oversee the production of standards, but not to do the actual work of creating those standards. Those roles are filled by volunteers, who are, in turn, employees or consultants paid by the standards body's corporate members.

That means that at an organization like the W3C (the World Wide Web Consortium, the body that sets standards for web browsers), the committees that write the standards are typically staffed by paid employees working on behalf of the largest tech companies.

After all, a company like Alphabet (Google's parent company) employs 150,000 people, so tasking a couple dozen of them with ensuring that web standards are favorable to Google's commercial interests isn't much of a burden.

Major firms' "volunteers" fill the majority of roles in standards committees: they are the moderators, chairs, co-chairs, secretaries and editors. Swelling their numbers are representatives from funded startups, whose investors pay for a handful of employees to work on standards that might benefit their future product plans (these startup employees often perform these duties on a part-time basis).

Beyond these core constituencies, standards committees sometimes include representatives from "civil society"—nonprofits and universities, generally. These are almost always part-timers, save for the odd semi-retired elder statesperson who has an honorary chair or advisory role at a civil society group and represents them full-time on standardization.

Standards bodies walk a fine line between remaining solvent and remaining relevant. A standards body that allows unlimited corporate influence may publish standards that no one adopts.

A hot area for the past three decades has been "patent ambushes"—when a corporate member of a standards committee pushes to ensure that its own technology is integrated into the standard, not revealing that it had filed a patent on those techniques until *after* the standard is published and the rest of the industry has invested in tooling up to make standards-conforming widgets.

The ambusher waits until other companies have passed the point of no return, then reveals the patent and announces that anyone who wishes to proceed with production of standards-conforming widgets will have to pay a toll to do so, in the form of a patent license royalty.

Even under the moral criteria of corporate America, this is a scummy trick, and so standards bodies have developed all kinds of gimmicks to prevent it: some (like the W3C) insist that all members must offer free licenses to patents that overlap with the standards they help create. Others require all members to pool their patents, then extract a "fair, reasonable and non-discriminatory" royalty from anyone who wants to implement the standard.

Patent ambushes are against the rules, but other forms of standards capture are fair game: for example, if the chair, co-chair and secretary all come from a single company (or a duopoly), that's fine, despite the fact that this means that the largest companies are literally setting the agenda.

This is obviously an invitation to standards capture, but it's hard to see how it could be otherwise. Say participation on a standards committee was limited to a single representative from each company—one Facebooker, one academic, one activist, one Googler.

When it comes time to produce proposals for the group, the Facebooker can muster a team—perhaps a few people, perhaps dozens, perhaps hundreds—to draft with them. When it's time to critique others' proposals, once again, the Facebooker or Googler can do the same.

I'm not saying that it's impossible to write good standards. A lot of the time, Facebook will want one thing and Google will want the opposite and the disagreement will go a long way to neutralizing the giants' attempts to tilt standards to parochial ends. What's more, the engineers who work on standards for the tech giants enjoy a lot of personal leeway because they have highly specialized skill sets and experience, and are given free rein to do good, solid work on standards where their employer does not have a dog in the fight.

But when the giants all want a standard kinked in a way that benefits them at the expense of the rest of the world, they're almost certainly going to get their way.

Here's an example of how this goes:

In 2000, there was a highly contested US election that ultimately went to the Supreme Court, which, in *Bush v. Gore*, decided that George W. Bush, who had lost the popular vote, was the winner. That led to Congress passing the Help America Vote Act, which mandated the creation of voting machine standards.

The Institute of Electrical and Electronics Engineers (IEEE)—one of the world's most respected standards bodies—took up the project of standardizing voting machines, gathering representatives from all the leading voting machine vendors. Sure, these were the companies whose machines had made such a mess out of the 2000 election, but they were also the world's leading experts on voting machines, right?

The committee—IEEE P-1583—quickly determined that creating a new standard for voting machines was too much work and would take too long to conclude, if the machines were to be ready for the upcoming elections.

So the committee—again, a committee composed primarily of representatives from the companies that made the defective voting machines the standard was supposed to replace—decided to create a "descriptive standard"; that is, the committee would literally describe all the existing (defective) voting machines, and say, "Any machine that matches any of these descriptions complies with the standard."

I was working for the Electronic Frontier Foundation when this happened, and we made a huge stink. A lot of our members were also IEEE members, and the resulting embarrassment led to the committee abandoning its work. A win, sure—but twenty years later, there's still no effective standard for secure voting machines.

Still, let's not be nihilists. Assume for the sake of argument that we can get a legislature or regulator to pass an interop mandate, and then we can draft a good interop standard that can be put in place.

We've still got a problem: cheating.

Let's say we force Facebook to allow third parties to connect to its service, so that people who leave Facebook can continue their individual and group conversations with the friends, family, communities and customers they left behind.

That connection—commonly called an Application Program Interface, or API—is a powerful tool for interoperators and the users they serve, but it's also a powerful weapon for identity thieves, fraudsters and wreckers. Subtle defects in this API could allow malicious parties posing as interoperators to siphon millions or even billions of users' data out of Facebook, or to create undetectable forged messages containing malicious links, or simply send so much data that Facebook slows down or even crashes.

Facebook already devotes substantial engineering resources to detecting and interdicting this kind of activity. We would not want the company to be any less diligent in guarding an interoperability API than they are in protecting other interfaces to their system.

But this brings up a serious conflict. Today, when Facebook locks down an account, or takes a server offline, or shuts down a back-end system its engineers suspect of being compromised, it's because it has a bona fide reason to think that something bad is going on.

However, if Facebook were to freeze a hypothetical mandatory API that its rivals depended on to provide services that made it easy for Facebook's users to quit the service and take their business elsewhere, could we ever be certain that the threat was real, and not just a pretext that allows Facebook to destabilize a rival?

How can we tell when Facebook shuts down a competitor out of an abundance of well-founded caution, and when Facebook shuts down that competitor in order to make it less useful and thus less attractive to Facebook users who had been contemplating a disloyal defection from Facebook to a new company?

The problem here is that Facebook—and other tech giants—operate highly specialized, bespoke server infrastructure, and to a first approximation everyone who understands how it works is an employee of the company that owns it. Yes, a court or regulator could send a swarm of technicians to descend on Facebook's data centers to perform a forensic investigation and determine whether a shutdown was warranted or pretextual.

But even if they determine that the shutdown was bogus, Facebook will doubtless claim innocence. That sets up a battle of dueling experts before the courts or a regulator, and it's the kind of technical battle that can drag out for years.

In the meantime, Facebook can shut down its rivals again and again and again. It can create an operating environment that's so chaotic and unreliable that its ex-users return to Facebook, and its current users give up any hope of leaving.

In other words, pretextual API shutdowns are just another means of intimidating users, entrepreneurs and investors into leaving Facebook to dominate its ever-expanding niche, teaching them the lesson that you can't win a bet against Big Tech.

Look, all this stuff—standardization meetings and forensic examinations of firewall errors—is *supremely* dull. It combines the thrill of bookkeeping with the excitement of Robert's *Rules of Order*. Merely paying attention to it is a trial, and many of us are literally cognitively incapable of tuning into it for more than a few minutes before our minds start to wander.

It is *precisely* because this stuff is so dull that it is so dangerous. The largest companies in the world hire squadrons of people whose neurology is wired for this stuff, people who are capable of producing—or closely reading—thousand-page technical specifications. This superpower allows them to hide all kinds of ugly stuff in the fine print.

In Dana Clare's *Phoebe and Her Unicorn* cartoons, a little girl called Phoebe has a unicorn for a friend, who is never noticed by the adults in Phoebe's life. That's not because the unicorn—whose name is Marigold Heavenly Nostrils—is invisible or anything. Rather, Marigold can project a *Shield of Boringness*, making herself so dull that other people's eyes slide right over her, and, if they do happen to notice her, they forget about her immediately and forever.

This deep procedural stuff—wrangles over standards and arguments over the true meaning of an Intrusion Detection System's warnings—has a prodigious shield of boringness. It is a powerful defense against public scrutiny. It's hard enough to even understand the underlying technical questions, but when the arguments themselves are long, tedious, technical and highly abstract, you can get away with nearly anything.

In light of that, how can we bring interoperability to Big Tech, and thus free its hostages? How can we win against the Shield of Boringness?

6

Adversarial Interop: Guerrilla Warfare and Reverse Engineering

Recall the story of Steve Jobs and the iWork suite: Microsoft had locked in billions of computer users with its proprietary, non-interoperable Microsoft Office file formats, which could only be read and written reliably by the Microsoft Office programs, which meant that Microsoft got to act as a kind of gatekeeper for the entire world of workplace and "productivity" computing.

This presented a problem for Apple. The version of Office that Microsoft offered for the Mac was insultingly terrible, and often incapable of reading and writing Office files created on Windows. That meant that Mac users were effectively cut off from the vast majority of computer users, who used Microsoft Windows (the US Department of Justice found that Microsoft commanded 95 percent of the operating system market).

Actually it was worse: Office for the Mac *sometimes* worked. You could share a file with a Windows-using colleague for edits, receive it back, make further edits and return it to the colleague for approval—only to find that neither of you could read the file any longer, or that it had become partially corrupted and garbled.

Somehow, Microsoft managed to engineer an intermittent reward schedule for Mac users that held out the fiendish temptation of a slot machine, that maybe this time you'd get lucky and finish your project without losing the files you'd been working on for days or weeks or months.

Apple was at the mercy of Microsoft, a company that the DoJ had successfully prosecuted for illegal bullying tactics in pursuit of a monopoly—which is to say, mercy was in short supply at Microsoft.

Steve Jobs didn't go on bent knee to Bill Gates and beg for a better version of Office for Mac. Instead, he tasked some of his programmers to reverse engineer the Office file formats.

"Reverse engineering" is a time-honored and important guerrilla tactic in all technological struggles. Its meaning is well captured by its name: reverse engineering takes place when a technologist deeply probes a finished product or service to determine how it works, and also how to change or replicate the way it works.

In 2008, archaeologists from Cardiff University subjected an odd relic to modern instruments. The relic was a barnacle-encrusted fused lump recovered from a Grecian shipwreck in 1901 near the island of Antikythera. Archaeologists had long known that this artifact, dated to the second century BCE, contained a gear, but beyond that, it remained a mystery.

Those Cardiff archaeologists, led by Mike Edmunds and Tony Freeth, put this fused lump in a state-of-the-art computerized x-ray tomography machine, and discovered that the lump didn't just have one gear—it had many. Puzzling over it, they realized that before this thing spent a couple thousand years at the bottom of the Mediterranean, it had been a computer—a hand-cranked device used for astronomical prediction.

They figured this out by looking at the gadget: how many teeth the gears had and how they meshed—imagining what the gadget would do if it were still in condition to be cranked to life.

This is reverse engineering: puzzling over the choices some other engineer, one whom you may know little or nothing about, one who may have given no thought at all to how the people of the future would understand and maintain their work. Indeed, that engineer might have even been hostile to future attempts to understand and alter their work—think of the designers who set traps in ancient burial sites to hold off grave robbers.

But you don't have to go all the way back to antiquity to find examples of reverse engineering. If you've ever renovated a room in your home and found a higgeldy-piggeldy of wires in the walls, or a snakes' nest of HVAC ductwork overhead, you know what it's like to work backward from an artifact to divine the intent of its maker.

Steve Jobs's reverse engineers likely knew their Microsoft rivals, at least in general terms. The industry was small then, and Silicon Valley was an even more incestuous affair than it is today, filling its ranks by drawing on the same handful of technical universities. It's possible the Apple employees who turned their hands to reverse engineering Microsoft Office had been taught by the same professors as the Microsoft engineers they were doing battle with. It's possible they even shared a class.

So these Apple engineers had a sound foundation to understand how their counterparts at Microsoft had designed their file formats and even what kinds of traps they might have set to foil reverse engineers. They were able to put themselves in the mindset of the programmers who designed and maintained Microsoft Office, just as archaeologists today strive to imagine the intent and techniques of the millennia-dead inventor of the Antikythera mechanism.

Reverse engineering is part of life everywhere and always. It is a core human experience. The very act of wondering "What did she mean by that?" is an act of reverse engineering: casting yourself into the place of some other person and trying to understand their motives and actions.

Reverse engineering is at the core of *adversarial* interoperability—the kind of interoperability that is undertaken against the wishes of the originators of some product or service. If your friend makes a confusing statement, you can ask them to clarify and trust their reply. If your enemy says something confusing, you *can* ask what they meant by it, but you won't know if the answer is trustworthy. Instead, you must gather information about how they act, what they have said to others, and how they have acted in the past. You can't ask them for clarity, you must *take it*.

A note on terminology here: "adversarial interoperability" is a phrase that only a wonk could love. It's hard to say, hard to spell, and its acronym (AI) is already taken. After brainstorming with my colleagues at the Electronic Frontier Foundation for a better name, we came up with "Competitive Compatibility," or comcom. "Comcom" is everything "adversarial interoperability" isn't: short, easy to say, punchy and easy to spell. I'll use "comcom" interchangeably with "adversarial interoperability."

Not all reverse engineering is adversarial (the plumber who turned your pipes into an MC Escher painting didn't want to obfuscate their workings, they just wanted to solve a series of immediate problems in locally expedient ways). But all comcom starts with reverse engineering.

Hardware engineers might tear down a device, examining the components inside it, googling its serial number and locating the manufacturer's spec sheets. They might connect a terminal to a controller and send it commonly used commands and examine the output—like a carpenter thumps your wall to find the studs, or like a doctor thumps your chest to check the quality of your breathing. They might carefully remove the top layers of resin from chips and examine the microcircuitry, or put them in an electron-tunneling microscope, or send them out-of-spec voltages and see what kinds of glitches they can induce.

A software reverse engineer might also send random inputs to a program to see how it breaks, or deliberately induce crashes in order to inspect the error logs they produce, or open the temporary files a program generates while it is running to see what kinds of notes it leaves for itself.

The software reverse engineer can inspect the contents of the computer's memory while the program is running, or they can go one better and run the program inside *another* program.

As previously discussed, all computers possess an irreducible, unavoidable characteristic called "universality"—the only computer we know how to build is the computer that can run every program we can write, the Turing Complete Universal von Neumann Machine.

One fascinating type of program is the *virtual machine* (VM): this is a program that simulates the action of a hardware processor. There are virtual machine programs that can simulate the functioning of nearly every processor ever invented. Because computing power increases so steeply, a modern computer is apt to be thousands or even millions of times faster than the computers you used a decade or two ago.

This means that VMs can run as fast—or even *much* faster—than the original computers they are re-creating. For example, when I send my consumer-grade personal laptop to oldweb .today, I can run a complete 1990s-era Macintosh computer in a browser window, loading up the old Mac System 7 (an operating system I once spent endless hours maintaining, running on a series of computers that cost a lot more than my laptop and ran at a fraction of its speed). Not only that, I can open half a dozen tabs and run a virtual 1990s-era Mac in each one of those tabs. My computer can do this without even needing to run the fan. It literally doesn't break a sweat.

Software reverse engineering often makes heavy use of VMs, because while a VM can faithfully reproduce a piece of hardware, it can also reproduce that old hardware in subtly altered ways: for example, a VM can be modified to give its master access to all the contents of its memory. You can intercept and inspect, block or alter every bit the programs in the VM try to send out over the internet. Every instruction in its processor can be inspected or altered, run one step at a time, forward *and* backward.

Talented reverse engineers aren't above making their own tools to do this, but generally they don't need to: there is a well-developed, well-maintained set of powerful, well-documented, easy-to-use tools for reverse engineering.

That might surprise you, but consider this: the way that security engineers defeat malicious software—ransomware worms, viruses that steal your data or spy through your webcam—is by reverse engineering it.

In 2017, a new ransomware worm swept across the internet. Dubbed WannaCry, this malicious program used defects in your browser and operating system to install itself on your computer. Then it would laboriously encrypt every file on your hard drive, permanently deleting the unencrypted copies as it went. Wanna-Cry was exceptionally virulent, and it swept the world, locking up everything from personal computers to critical hospital systems.

There's a reason WannaCry was so powerful: it was a lab leak. The US National Security Agency (NSA)—a secretive federal agency tasked with securing Americans' computers against foreign adversaries—had discovered defects in Microsoft Windows and then, rather than telling Microsoft about these bugs, kept them secret. The NSA wanted to be able to use these defects to attack its adversaries.

Then, hackers (believed to be working for the North Korean military) penetrated the NSA's computers and leaked many of their cyberweapons, including a Microsoft Windows defect called "EternalBlue." The criminals behind WannaCry married an older piece of ransomware to EternalBlue, creating a powerful hybrid.

WannaCry was hard to study. Security researchers set up "honey pots"—insecure VMs inside secure computers, dangled out there on the open web as a temptation for malicious software like WannaCry. But every time they managed to catch a WannaCry infection in one of their VM observatories, it would go dormant, sullenly refusing to run itself and, in so doing, reveal its workings to the researchers who'd captured it.

A young British security researcher named Marcus "Malware-Tech" Hutchins figured out what was going on. He observed that on infected machines, WannaCry tried to contact a web server at the domain iuqerfsodp9ifjaposdfjhgosurijfaewrwergwea.com. At first, he thought that perhaps this was the "command and control" server—the hub that infected computers phoned home to for new marching orders.

But when he checked, iuqerfsodp9ifjaposdfjhgosurijfaewrwe rgwea.com wasn't even registered. Curious, he spent $10 to register the domain and put up a simple web server at that address.

And then … every WannaCry worm in the world *stopped*.

It turned out that the iuqerfsodp9ifjaposdfjhgosurijfaewrwe rgwea.com domain was actually used by WannaCry to figure out if it was running inside a VM—and thus likely to be under inspection by its adversary, the wily security researcher. You see, security researchers routinely configure their workbench VMs to intercept and reply to any internet connection the programs in the VM try to initiate—that is, no matter what number the virus tries to call, the VM answers "Hello?" and listens to what the malware says next, to glean intelligence about its operations.

WannaCry's authors realized that this could be used to *detect*

VMs: simply initiate a connection to a server that doesn't exist, and if you reach it, you *know* you're inside a crystal prison where the all-powerful jailer is manipulating reality itself.

So when Hutchins stood up a web server at iuqerfsodp9ifja posdfjhgosurijfaewrwergwea.com, every WannaCry infection in the world initiated its periodic, "Am I in a VM?" test, got an answer back from his server, and immediately went into cold sleep to guard its secrets from the world.

Once word got out, Hutchins's web server immediately became the target of sustained, massive floods of garbage traffic in an attempt to overwhelm it and knock it offline. But other security researchers rallied to Hutchins's side and helped shore up the server. So long as that server was live, every WannaCry instance in the world would stay dormant, and that didn't just mean that they couldn't attack more hospitals and businesses and city governments—it *also* meant that they couldn't receive a software update that told them not to rely on checking in with iuqerfso dp9ifjaposdfjhgosurijfaewrwergwea.com before running.

The story of MalwareTech vs. WannaCry is a spectacular example of something very common: one engineer made something, so another engineer figured out how it worked, took it apart and made it do something very different.

Indeed, the NSA—whose EternalBlue cyberweapon was the delivery system for WannaCry's ransomware encryption tool— likely used similar tools and techniques to discover and exploit the flaw in Microsoft Windows that was weaponized to make EternalBlue. That is, NSA engineers probably put a copy of Windows inside a VM, tormented it in all sorts of imaginative ways and observed closely how it reacted.

Everyone relies on comcom tools, in other words: engineers who make malicious software *and* engineers who fight malicious software alike. Not just them, either: archivists who need to preserve old programs or read old data, or IT workers who need to nurse along an old, mission-critical system whose manufacturer is long defunct.

This may seem like technological guerrilla warfare, but it is par for the course in product design, systems maintenance and security. It is a normal part of any technologist's life.

Big companies that have cooked up extractive, monopolistic business models—from forcing you to buy expensive printer ink, to forcing you to use their app store to add features to your phone, to forcing you to stay inside their surveillance perimeter in order to socialize with your friends and family—like to stress all the ways that "bad guys" do adversarial interoperability.

They blithely conflate the engineer who figures out how to finesse a printer into accepting cheap ink refills with the criminal who shuts down all the IT systems in a cancer ward, and demand that Something Be Done.

The argument works. Over the years, felony contempt of business model has gone from being a sarcastic joke to a serious doctrine. Abusive companies used some of the vast sums they extracted from their customers by dint of their ability to lock in users and lock out reverse engineers to promote legal theories that allow companies with deep pockets to use the law—not technology—to ward off interoperators.

These new laws present a kind of thicket of overlapping legal shields that can be deployed by companies with the millions needed to present them to a judge. Taken singly, each of these laws seems reasonable and well designed, with exceptions and carve-outs that serve as escape hatches to ensure that the laws don't interfere with legitimate activity.

But with a sufficiently large legal budget, a canny company can use one law to plug up the escape valves in another, and a third law to plug up the holes in *that* one, and so on, creating an impregnable legal wall that allows dominant corporations to decide who is allowed to compete with them, and how.

For example, take trademark law. Trademark is often lumped in with copyright and patent as a form of "IP," but in truth, trademark is a completely different sort of system. Copyright and patent are exclusive rights (over expression, in the case of copyright; and ideas, in the case of patents). Lawmakers give companies patents and copyrights to reward and incentivize them to create new creative works and useful inventions.

A copyright or a patent is, fundamentally, a license to sue others who duplicate your products. That license is dangled before inventors and creators, as a carrot to tempt them to set aside their other pressing needs and devote themselves to invention and creation.

Not so trademark. Trademark has nothing to do with incentives. It is not a reward. It doesn't even really belong to the company that holds the trademark—the company is merely its custodian.

At root, trademark is a system of *consumer protection*. The purpose of a trademark is to prevent the public from being deceived when they buy a product or service. Trademark is there to make sure that when you walk into a McDonald's restaurant and order a Big Mac, you're in a real McD's and getting a real Big Mac.

Trademark empowers companies to act *on behalf of their customers*: companies are empowered to use the courts to shut down copycats who behave in a deceptive manner—who market their products and services in a way that is "likely to give rise to confusion."

If someone opens a fake McDonald's restaurant and starts serving fake Big Macs, McDonald's can use the courts to shut them down with trademark claims, but not to protect *McDonald's* —trademark lets them do this to protect *you* from deception.

It's a subtle but important distinction. Copyright lets rights-holders defend their own economic interests against competitors who misappropriate their works; trademark lets sellers protect their *customers'* economic interests against competitors who seek to trick those customers.

The corollary is that trademark does *not* protect companies from rivals who use their marks in ways that *don't* deceive their customers, even if that ends up hurting the companies that hold the trademarks.

That means you can open a restaurant called "Better Than McDonald's" and serve a sandwich called the "Better than a Big Mac"—or, as is more common, you can sell a charger cable and advertise "Works with an Apple iPhone." So long as no one is being tricked into thinking they're eating a Big Mac at McDonald's or charging their phone with an Apple cable, no one's trademark is being violated.

Enter Apple.

Apple is one of the leading opponents of interoperability. Their mobile devices—iPhones, iPads and iPods—are designed to block third-party app stores (Apple collects billions in commissions from its own App Store, which charges sellers a 15-to-30 percent transaction fee on every penny earned by their apps), as well as third-party parts needed to repair Apple devices.

At the start of 2019, Apple CEO Tim Cook warned his shareholders that Apple was facing a serious threat: its customers were holding onto their mobile devices for longer periods, rather than replacing them every year or two.

Cook's shareholder letter came at the tail end of a twelve-month corporate killing spree, during which time Apple had led a coalition of manufacturers that successfully lobbied against eighteen different state-level right-to-repair laws that would have forced Apple to supply independent repair depots with parts, manuals and access to the error codes generated by Apple customers' devices.

Getting rid of independent repair would be great for Apple's bottom line: for one thing, the company could set the fees for labor and service just below the point where a customer will say, "To hell with it, I'll just get a different phone."

But more than that, controlling repair lets Apple control the cadence of your replacement of your devices, because it lets Apple decide when a phone can be repaired at all—and, unlike an independent repair depot, which might declare your phone beyond repair and offer you a nice deal on an Android phone or a used iPhone, Apple can control the whole end-of-life experience, declaring your phone dead and offering you a trade-in on this year's iPhone model.

This is a great deal for Apple, and not just because the corporation gets to force an upgrade, but also because it gives Apple control over the disposal of your ex-phone. Apple—uniquely among major manufacturers—has a policy of shredding devices consigned to it for recycling, which ensures that no parts can be harvested from old phones and used to patch up other devices.

But even with this "recycling" scheme, lots of Apple devices reach the end of their lives without being turned in to Apple for annihilation. These were distributed around the Pacific Rim, where low-wage workers break them down and harvest their parts, which are collected, packaged and shipped back to the

USA (this is a surprisingly common practice—a lot of third-party printer ink cartridges use "security chips" extracted from official, manufacturer-supplied cartridges).

These are real Apple parts, tested and fit for service. They embody tons of conflict minerals and immortal plastics, as well as gigawatts of energy. These aren't just diverted from a landfill when they're rescued and sent back stateside—they also rescue phones from the scrapheap, as independent technicians, working with third-party manuals (like the ones that iFixit makes through tearing down and reverse engineering Apple devices) to fix Americans' phones.

This is a big problem for Apple. Honestly, you couldn't ask for a more flagrant case of felony contempt of business model. An iPhone that is fixed by an independent technician is bad for Apple's shareholders in so many ways: first, because they lose out on the windfall profits they'd receive from charging for brand-new parts and labor; second, because they lose on the chance to coerce an upgrade out of a customer by declaring a phone to be beyond repair; and finally, because they lose the opportunity to offer a trade-in on the phone that keeps the customer locked into Apple hardware (independent repair shops will often cheerfully offer a trade-in credit that customers can apply to used or new phones from any manufacturer, and will assist in moving Apple data to Android and vice versa).

In other words, independent repair is a powerful means to transfer value from Apple's shareholders to Apple's customers, and that is a problem for Tim Cook, whose job as CEO is to ensure that the value flows to the company's owners.

Enter trademark. If you have an iPhone handy and you want to see something few people have ever seen, crack it open. You can do this by microwaving a beanbag and wrapping it around the phone to melt the glue and then using a "spudger" tool to pry the case apart, or you can opt to use Apple's own kit, which weighs 80 pounds and is shipped to you in two Pelican cases, which you have to ship back to the company or forfeit a $1,200 credit-card hold. Or you can just hit it with a hammer (wear eye- and hand-protection!).

Once you're inside the phone's guts, get a magnifying glass and start checking out the parts. They're precisely manufactured to extremely fine tolerances—and they are engraved with minuscule (and even *microscopic*) Apple logos.

As noted, almost no one will ever see these—they are not there for human consumption. They exist for the purposes of invoking trademark. Apple claims that anyone who harvests these parts and ships them to the United States is violating its trademarks. They argue that the ant-sized Apple logos on those parts are a signal to consumers: *this is an Apple product, and will be as reliable and well made as any other Apple product.*

They argue that because the reclamation and refurbishment process produces parts that might be almost undetectably less reliable than using factory-fresh parts, prospective purchasers are being deceived as to the quality of these parts, even though they are being sold as "refurbished." This, says Apple, is a special kind of trademark violation called "tarnishment," by which they mean something weird and circular like: "Apple makes a high-quality product; when that product is refurbished by randos, it might become a low-quality product. Consumers who are burned by this will come to associate the Apple logo—which we engraved in miniature on all those parts—with low-quality goods and will therefore struggle to make accurate assessments of our products in the marketplace."

So, they say, to prevent consumers from being confused, they argue that US Customs should seize and destroy these refurbished parts at the US border. And the whole thing turns on the existence of those infinitesimal Apple logos, engraved on the parts.

Apple's use of trademark to clamp down on refurbished parts is an example of how clever lawyers can deploy multiple, overlapping legal theories to create impregnable felony-contempt-of-business-model regimes:

Apple uses patent to prevent the independent manufacture of some parts; it uses anti-circumvention to prevent the independent installation of other parts; it uses contractual arrangements with recyclers to ensure that most used phones are not broken down for parts; it uses trademark to block the re-importation of parts that have escaped the recyclers' shredders.

This is what I mean when I say there's a "thicket" of laws that stand in the way of interoperability. Reforming any one of these laws would make a difference, but to actually clear the way for interop, we need to reform all of them. But that's a tall order.

7

Jam Tomorrow: Life after We Seize the Means of Computation

"The rule is, jam to-morrow and jam yesterday—but never jam to-day."

—The Red Queen, *Through the Looking Glass and What Alice Found There*, by Lewis Carroll

Once, we had interop, and with it, all the choice and empowerment that comes from being able to tell a tech company to go fuck itself if it mistreats you.

Today, interop only exists to the extent that the dominant companies deign to permit it.

Tomorrow? Tomorrow, we might get interop, and with it, a precious prize: technological self-determination, which is the right not just to choose what your technology does, but whom it does it *for* and whom it does it *to*.

For this chapter, I'd like you to suspend your disbelief for a moment and consider what we're fighting for. (Don't worry, in the *next* chapter I'll tell you how we get it.)

Here are three visions of an interoperable life.

Life Doesn't Have to Zuck

At the time of this writing, Mark Zuckerberg is the unelected, unaccountable, absolute czar of the digital lives of about 4 billion people. He didn't earn that job—he bought it. When companies like Instagram and WhatsApp arrived on the scene with superior products that Facebook users preferred and started to leave Facebook for, Mark Zuckerberg threw his shareholders' money around, buying both companies for a total of $23 billion. Zuck's access to the capital markets meant that you couldn't escape from his custody—if you left his walled garden, he'd track you down to whatever new service you found and buy it and build a wall around it.

This is a classic monopoly play. It's why nearly everything in the grocery store is made by either Unilever or Procter & Gamble. If an independent manufacturer manages to create a successful product despite the duopoly's exclusive grocery-store deals, access to eye-height shelf space and predatory pricing, then that company will be bought out by P&G or Unilever.

When they do buy out that beloved local brand, they'll hold a press conference, and at that presser, a duopoly spokesperson will say, "We—who make nearly all the cookies for sale in America —bought out this amazing cookie manufacturer because we know our customers value choice."

That's Zuck's story: we bought Insta and WhatsApp because we know you value choice, and we want to give it to you.

What if you could make a choice that *really* mattered: the choice not to do business with Zuck, or Facebook, or Meta?

By and large, Facebook users hate being Facebook users. Facebook users mistrust the company, with good reason. And yet, they keep using it (not all of them, Facebook has been slowly but surely losing users, especially in America, but it still has more than 3 billion regular users).

The most common explanation for the fact that people who don't like Facebook keep using it is that Facebook is somehow "addictive." It's easy to see why, because addicts are famous for saying that they hate their addictions but feel powerless to give them up. There's an obvious parallel between the Facebook user who logs in for the tenth time in a day while muttering, "God, I hate Facebook," and the chain smoker who lights their next smoke off the butt of the last one and declares, "Ugh, I hate these cancer sticks."

But scientists who study addiction are *very* skeptical of this framing. While the underlying biology of addiction isn't terribly well understood, online services just don't seem capable of creating the same physiological changes as nicotine or heroin or alcohol.

If Facebook users who hate Facebook and use it anyway aren't addicted, then what explains that usage?

In short, Facebook *users* are why other Facebook users stick with the service. If you're on Facebook, chances are it's because there are friends, or community members, or family members, or customers, who are also on Facebook and you don't want to give them up.

What's more, *they're* on Facebook because *you're* there. It's a mutual hostage-taking situation. In theory, you could all decamp to another service—say, a standalone server running a free/open social media program like Mastodon or Diaspora.

But how would you organize that? It's very hard to get a group of friends to agree on what movie to see or where to eat dinner—getting several groups of friends and family members and strangers in groups you enjoy and customers you have no control over to all agree on another service and then to switch in unison? It's a tall order. Maybe an impossible one.

Economists call this a "collective action problem" and it's a specific kind of switching cost: to switch away from Facebook you must either figure out how to convince everyone you talk to on Facebook to switch with you (a high cost) or forfeit your relationship with them (also a high cost).

That's where interoperability comes in. Imagine if there were *lots* of services that provided Facebook-like features: private messaging, group chat and public groups, for starters. If these services could interoperate with Facebook, you could sign up with one of them and tell Facebook where you've moved to.

Facebook would let the new service import your group memberships and contact list, and it would automatically send messages addressed to you to the new service. Your groups— public and private—would have their own areas on the new service and you could read the messages other members posted there, and your replies would be synchronized with Facebook, so the group members who haven't left Facebook (yet) would be able to see them and reply to them.

This is called "federation," and as the name implies, it allows for lots of different services to connect with one another to create a large space made up of standalone servers run by independent entities, separated by semipermeable membranes.

The web is federated. There are lots of places that will host your web server, web service or webpage for you. You can buy space in a data center and install your own PC, or you can buy a virtual server from a cloud provider like Amazon Web Services, or you can buy a WordPress site from hundreds of companies.

The links you make on your website can refer to any page on any other website, and they can link to your pages. You can have policies about what you will link to—I generally don't link to anything on Facebook or Instagram, because, frankly, fuck them—and other sites can have policies that determine whether they will link to you. You can set up parts of your website behind a password or a paywall, and you can decide from moment to moment which parts are visible to the public and which parts are behind the wall.

Email is federated, too. You can set up your own email server (again, either by installing a physical server in a data center, or by renting a virtual server on a cloud service, or by paying for email hosting through a mail provider), or you can get an email address through your employer or school, or you can pay for an email address with a company like ProtonMail, or you can get free email from a service like Gmail.

All of these services can exchange email with one another. Even bitter rivals, like Apple and Facebook, can exchange email with each other. They all have different policies; some block emails with certain words or senders, others block whole servers or even whole countries' worth of servers.

Federated social media follows this pattern. You can join or launch a server and it can have its own moderation policies: some words or phrases or images might be automatically blocked, others might be blocked or tagged by human moderators. You might permit things that Facebook blocks, and you might block some things that Facebook allows (for example, you might decide that Donald Trump posting "When the looting starts, the shooting starts" has crossed a line and block all his messages thereafter—or you might decide that *nothing* posted by the president of the United States should *ever* be blocked. It's your choice).

You might also block whole servers based on their policies. Say you run a community for breast cancer "previvors"—people who carry the BRCA gene or other genetic markers that indicate a high risk for breast cancer. You could decide, as a group, that you will not entertain discussions of "alternative" medicine and block any server that permits or encourages talk of crystal healing, reiki and other non–evidence-based therapies.

A user of that blocked server who tried to join your group would get a message saying they would have to sign up for another server if they wanted to participate. They might choose to maintain two accounts, or switch all their activities to the new server, or they might decide not to join your group after all —they might go hunting for a group that was more tolerant of pseudoscience and spirituality.

Federated social media devolves moderation choices to the groups they affect, and allows those groups to block or welcome other groups based on their own choices.

It's likely that this will *work* better than the centralized moderation policies that Facebook or Twitter hand down, because the moderation will be carried out by people who understand the context of the community.

Take the problem of racial slurs. Today, online communities where people of color gather to commiserate about the racist slurs they encounter in the world have a problem: moderators from big social media companies have been ordered to delete racial abuse and block the users who post it. These moderators sometimes struggle to distinguish between racial abuse and *discussions* of racial abuse—that is, they are prone to confusing, "You dirty n-word!" and "I can't believe that racist asshole called me a dirty n-word!" When they mix these up, the *target* of the abuse can have their account suspended or terminated (Mark Zuckerberg told the US Congress that they'd solve this with automated moderation tools, but these robot moderators make these mistakes far more often than humans do).

Moderators drawn from the community are less likely to commit this error, because they have the context to understand the difference between engaging in racial abuse and describing that abuse after the fact.

What's more, the toxic trolls who make a vocation out of abusing people online will have a harder time slipping past the radar of a community-based moderator than they will when it comes to mass-scale corporate moderation.

Social media companies have an impossible conundrum. They can empower their moderators to remove content that *feels* like it crosses a line, but if they do that, then the "justice system" of the platform will be a hodgepodge of decisions resulting from gut checks. It's "the rule of man," not "the rule of law."

On the other hand, if social media companies compose detailed rules about which speech is permissible and which speech is beyond the pale, these rules are easy to game. If a social media company crisply defines "harassment" based on a set of bright-line tests that low-wage moderators must apply to every piece of suspected harassment, then dedicated trolls can carefully work out the contours of these rules through trial and error, using throwaway accounts to determine what kinds of slurs and behavior are over the line. Then the trolls can invent a whole range of tactics that go *right up to that line*, tactics that are almost-but-not-quite-harassment, and stick to those.

If a moderator decides that the almost-but-not-quite harassment is a rules violation, the troll can cite chapter-and-verse and maybe get off. Meanwhile, for the *targets* of harassment, almost-but-not-quite-harassment is indistinguishable from harassment.

Indeed, given the rich tapestry of ways in which people can make one another miserable, a rules-based approach to preventing unpleasant behavior will never be complete. Worse still, every new amendment and codicil becomes another rule that harassers can accuse their victims of violating.

In other words, the less specific the rules are, the more the trolls can get away with.

But also, the *more* specific the rules are, the more trolls can get away with, and the harder it is for their victims to answer back without getting censured, suspended or kicked off the system altogether.

The problem isn't merely that Facebook and other large systems underinvest in moderation and are indifferent to the harms experienced by the users of their services—it's also that no amount of investment and no amount of caring would actually solve the problem of dedicated trolls, griefers and harassers. Moderate a lot or a little, be specific or general, it doesn't matter—the trolls will win.

But not if the moderation is done by the community itself. At least, not necessarily. Members of a community can understand its nuances and norms, and that gives them a fighting chance of resolving thorny conflicts and sorting malicious pot-stirring from genuine ire.

I'm not saying that communities that moderate themselves will always get it right. I'm saying that communities moderated by distant, unaccountable moderators will never get it right—and that communities that moderate themselves have a chance of getting it right.

What's more, when they get it wrong, their users will have options. Federation and interoperability means that community members who chafe at the rules set by the majority can take their data, their contact lists and their opinions and join (or create) another server with rules they like better. They can exchange messages with the friends they left behind, and fork off a rival community with policies that suit them.

There's an App (Store) for That

In 1907, the Victor Record company ran full-page newspaper ads warning its customers not to play Victor records on third-party record players. In 1917, the Motion Picture Patents Company sued to prevent its rivals' films from being run through its projectors (the Supreme Court ruled against the company).

The urge to control which media your customers can play on

your device is an old one. Doubtless there were swordsmiths who insisted that their sabers could only be carried in an official, authorized sheath and stone-ax makers who insisted that their weapons only be assembled using their own specially prepared sinew.

Inevitably, these demands are wrapped in righteous claims that the company is only looking out for your best interests. The reason your printer company is forcing you to use its ink is that it's afraid you'll be fooled into buying an inferior third-party ink and your precious photos and documents will fade. It has nothing to do with the fact that the company's own ink comes at a 10 million percent markup.

That's a coincidence, and you should be ashamed of yourself for thinking that they would deploy all that ink-locking technology for mere mercenary rent-seeking.

In the mid-1990s, video-game consoles switched from using proprietary cartridges to using CD-ROMs. That was a literal and figurative game-changer. Manufacturing a game cartridge required custom tooling and circuitry, and many cartridge designs included patented elements, and all this added up to a serious barrier to third parties that wanted to make their own cartridges for Atari, ColecoVision, Intellivision and Nintendo systems. That was good news for the companies that made the consoles: they could either monopolize the games that ran on their machines, or charge high fees to software developers who wanted to sell games for them.

But CD-ROMs are standardized technology, cheaply pressed in vast quantities in huge factories all over the world. Once Sega and Sony shipped consoles that used CD-ROMs, they opened the door to third parties making games and selling them directly to PlayStation and Sega Saturn owners, without cutting Sony and Sega in on a piece of the action.

These early CD-based consoles used software locks—digital rights management—to lock out third-party games. If your friend programmed a game for your PS One and burned it to a CD-ROM, your PS One would refuse to load it, because your friend couldn't replicate the cryptographic signatures that Sony used to reassure your console that the game in its belly was generating revenue for the company.

Naturally, Sony insisted that it was doing this for the good of the market. By preventing independent software houses from selling directly to PlayStation owners, Sony was serving as a *curator*, protecting its customers from cack-handed programmers who made inferior games.

Not only that, but Sony was *also* protecting those independent games companies. Sure, they had to pay exorbitant fees to have their games blessed by Sony, but they were also participating in a system that prevented copyright infringement, because pirates who duplicated those copyrighted games and burned them to CD-ROMs would be thwarted by Sony's DRM—its mechanisms for "digital rights management." Thus began a game of cat-and-mouse, as reverse engineers unraveled the games consoles' DRM and taught one another how to make homebrew games and backup copies (and yes, pirated games) that could pass the consoles' security checks. In response, console makers rolled out new DRM systems, but they were hamstrung by the primitive state of the 1990s internet—most of their customers didn't have broadband and could not run software updates for their consoles, so the games manufacturers couldn't easily update their systems to lock out unauthorized discs.

This was the backdrop for the passage of the Digital Millennium Copyright Act in 1998, and it's why Section 1201 of the DMCA bans *all* circumvention (that is, bypassing digital locks) rather than just those circumventions that lead to a copyright infringement.

It is no copyright infringement for me to write a game for your Sega and sell it to you so you can play it. The only thing this infringes upon is Sega's ability to interpose itself between me and you and siphon off money it didn't earn, leading to either lower creative wages for me, or higher prices for you, or both.

DMCA 1201 was designed to protect business models, not copyright—and while I've discussed innumerable models that it protects (monopolizing repair, or printer ink, or car parts), the meat and potatoes of DMCA 1201 is the games console racket —where the company that sells you a player gets to decide who can make the things it will play and take a cut of every one of those things.

A quarter-century later, that racket has gone viral. Amazon's Audible claims the right to decide who can make an audiobook player that can use the books it sells you, and Amazon's Kindle devices will only run software that is authorized by Amazon. Smart thermostats, smart speakers and smart toys all leave the factory locked to their makers' app stores.

All of these companies make the same claims as Sega: we're not locking you *in*, we're locking the bad guys *out*. The 30 percent take we cream off of every purchase you make isn't rent-seeking—it's *cost-recovery*, a modest commission that lets us pay our expert curators to ensure that the apps in our app store are high-quality, safe and secure.

This is an obvious ruse. Companies use their app store monopolies to lock out rivals that make apps that directly compete with their own, or, if they accept those apps, they can bury them on page 98,231 of the app store's listings. They claim their 30 percent cut is cost-recovery, but boast to their shareholders that it makes them billions in pure profit.

It's true that app stores *sometimes* serve to weed out bad apps and promote good ones, but even the best app stores inevitably get caught between their owners' commercial priorities and the desire to protect their customers.

Take the most famous app store, the Apple iOS App Store, which is the exclusive conduit for apps on Apple's iPhone, iPad and iPod. Apple rightly trumpets the privacy protections built into its app model; for example, in 2021 the company updated its devices so that merely by ticking a single box, iOS users could block *all* tracking for *all* apps, by default.

Ninety-six percent of iOS users chose to block tracking, a figure so high that I suspect the 4 percent that didn't block tracking were confused and ticked the wrong box.

Apple trumpets its privacy protections, and rightly so. A pro-privacy stance is rare in Big Tech, and Apple's design choices make for a hell of a comparison with, say, Facebook—who told its shareholders that Apple's blocking cost it *$10 billion* in the first year.

But Apple's privacy ethic is very ... *contingent*. Apple doesn't want to profit by invading your privacy for advertising, but that doesn't mean they won't invade your privacy when their business depends on it.

In 2017, the Chinese government instituted a ban on privacy tools like VPNs, which allow their users to evade the Chinese state's network-level censorship and surveillance. Apple complied. What's more, that decision involving Apple's App Store model—which blocks any software except those apps that Apple has blessed by making available through its App Store—meant that Chinese Apple customers had no ability to get privacy tools elsewhere.

Apple went on to install "backdoors" in its Chinese cloud servers, ensuring that Chinese military and police snoops could plunder any Chinese iPhone user's photos, notes, messages and other private information.

Chinese digital surveillance isn't about advertising—it's far more sinister. Advertisers may use surveillance data in an attempt to manipulate you into buying things you don't need, or trick you into taking actions that you don't intend. They may use surveillance troves to instill and prey on insecurities about your appearance or social status.

But the Chinese state's surveillance puts Apple customers in much graver danger, with losses more consequential than mere monetary drains or lingering neuroses about your skin or body or net worth. The Chinese state spies on Apple customers to determine which ones should be excluded from banking services, or access to intercity travel, or education or employment. The Chinese state uses the surveillance data that Apple helps it capture to determine which of Apple's customers should be imprisoned, which should be tortured and which should be executed.

Apple values privacy, but it balances its commitment to privacy against the interests of its shareholders. If Apple failed to comply with Chinese surveillance demands, it would have been kicked out of China. That would have cost the company access to the Chinese middle class, all 700 million–plus of them, and even more importantly, it would have cost Apple its access to Chinese manufacturing, forcing up the company's manufacturing bill with a costly move to another Pacific Rim sweatshop territory, like Vietnam.

The story of Apple's inconstant commitment to its users' privacy neatly illustrates what the cryptographer Bruce Schneier calls "feudal security."

Schneier compares the modern internet to feudal Europe, a half-wild place plagued by roving gangs of bandits who prey upon hardworking peasants. The peasants are all but defenseless on their own, but they can still protect themselves by allying themselves with a feudal warlord and moving into his fortress.

That fortress—Apple's iOS, Google's Android, Meta's Facebook or Microsoft's Exchange—is protected by high walls and frowning battlements and an army of skilled mercenaries who patrol them—these being the security experts on Big Tech's payrolls.

In exchange for our loyalty—and a share of the income we earn thanks to their protection—that warlord's mercenaries will defend us ... from the bandits.

But those mercenaries will not lift a finger to defend us *from the warlord* that pays them. If Apple—or Google, or Facebook, or Microsoft—decides that it is in its own self-interest to prey on us, or to allow someone else to do so, our defenders become our prison guards, and the fortress becomes a dungeon. Our protectors become our hostage-takers.

And to add insult to injury, they claim they're doing it for our own good. Just as printer manufacturers claim they lock us into their high-priced ink to protect us from having our family photos fade and blur, so do tech giants who cave to autocratic regimes. "We *could* pull out of China, but that would just punish our innocent Chinese users. Don't they deserve the elegance and pleasure of using Apple products?"

In Apple's defense, they by no means originated this nonsense; it's nearly the same claim Google made when it entered the Chinese market in 2006, agreeing to censor search results and surveil searchers for the Chinese government: "By exposing Chinese netizens to the excellence of Google search, we will inspire them to demand more of their own leaders."

(The experiment ended in 2010 when the Chinese government hacked numerous dissidents' Gmail accounts, shaking Google cofounder Sergey Brin, a Soviet refugee, who was conscience-stricken at his company's complicity in political oppression of the sort his own family had fled. He ordered the company out of China.)

App stores are an "attractive nuisance." The ability to control which software your customers can run fires the imagination of your corporate princelings, who immediately set to scheming about how they can use this control to make their own products succeed—by suppressing independent rivals and other "self-preferencing" activity. This same impulse occurs in the halls of power around the world, as the worst authoritarians, snoops and bullies in every government realize that if they can order you to remove an app, or force a specific app to the top of searches, they can turn you into an engine for executing their policies.

No one with half an ounce of sense can claim to have been surprised when the Chinese government ordered Apple to use its control over apps to expose its users to surveillance. The very instant Apple hung that gun over the mantelpiece in Act I, it roused a chorus clamoring that the gun would surely go off by Act III. Now that it has, there's no pleasure in saying "I told you so"—not while the Chinese state is using mobile surveillance data to decide who joins the million-plus prisoners in its concentration camps.

The grim lessons of the Chinese App Store illustrate the link between unfettered commercial ambition and state oppression.

In the United States, Congress consistently fails to pass comprehensive national privacy legislation in large part thanks to the lobbying of US police and intelligence services, who rely on their ability to subpoena or simply purchase commercial surveillance data as a means of doing an end-run around the legal niceties of search warrants.

In China, the state chooses to allow Apple to maintain its control over its App Store—despite the harm this visits upon Chinese domestic app makers, who must win the approval of a California corporation in order to secure approval for their software—because Apple's locked-down devices deliver a much more important benefit to the Chinese state, far more valuable than mere national self-determination on apps. By allowing Apple to determine which apps can—and can't—run on iOS devices, the Chinese state gains the power to control which apps Chinese people can use. They just have to order Apple to remove an app, and Apple's App Store will make the decision stick. Even if a Chinese user gets ahold of a program that's been banned in China, their Apple phone will refuse to run it.

Once again, it's not that companies *can't* use app stores to protect their customers from digital abuse—but app stores can also be a means of inflicting abuse.

What can we do about it? Well, for starters, we could withdraw the legal protections that Apple and other companies use to prevent other companies from creating their own app stores: anti-circumvention law, patents, trade secrecy, cybersecurity, contract ... the whole "thicket" of laws that block comcom.

We might also *require* dominant companies to allow for third-party app stores (as the EU will do with the Digital Markets Act and the United States may do with the Open App Markets Act). Or, if we don't want to go that far, there are some fascinating technical alternatives, like mandating full-featured browser engines.

A "browser engine" is a program that loads HTML (and JavaScript) and renders and/or executes it. At the time of this writing, the latest version of HTML is HTML5. While HTML has its origins as a "markup language" to help web authors control the display of words and pictures (for example, setting some text in italics, or padding the text around an image by 15 pixels), HTML5 is fully programmable. That is, it's a Turing Complete programming language, one that can be used to write any valid program.

That means that a browser engine that fully implements HTML5 can run any program, which means that anything an app can do, a fully implemented HTML5 browser engine can also do. That means that "web apps"—apps that are loaded inside a webpage—can do anything an app can do.

The specifications for web apps envision web apps as co-equal to apps installed via an app store. As designed, you could download a web app in a browser, then select "Save as app" and it would show up on your home screen as an icon, right next to all the other apps you've installed through the app store.

However, Apple does not allow any browser engines on iOS

except its own, WebKit. Whether you download Chrome, Edge, Firefox or Brave on your iOS device, you're not getting their browser engines—by Apple's order, these browsers all run on WebKit, making them functionally equivalent to Safari, Apple's default browser. WebKit does *not* implement all of HTML5— specifically, it does not fully implement the parts of the standard that would enable full-fledged web apps.

Hypothetically, Apple could offer different browser engines via its App Store, but it hasn't. Indeed, Apple has thus far categorically rejected such a possibility. The UK Competition and Markets Authority—probably the world's most high-tech competition regulator, with a permanent staff of eighty engineers and technologists devoted to understanding and producing detailed regulations for tech companies—has investigated this and sought comment on whether Apple should be forced to open iOS to alternative browser engines.

Apple objects strenuously to this proposal, arguing that WebKit is key to the safety and security of iOS users, and that third-party browser engines could contain security defects that expose Apple customers to privacy, financial and safety risks.

They're not wrong—a bad third-party browser engine, capable of reaching into an iPhone's storage, network connections and sensors (including its cameras, microphones and GPS), could indeed expose Apple customers to risk.

But they're not right, either. Apple's own browser engine, WebKit, is riddled with defects and is only desultorily maintained. It has been the source of numerous security issues, and because every iOS browser is built atop WebKit, these security issues can't be mitigated by switching to a different browser. Whether your iPhone is running Safari, Chrome, Edge, Firefox or Brave, it's actually running WebKit, and any exploits for WebKit are problems with any browser you might switch to.

Apple—and feudal warlords of the digital age—argue that they keep their customers safe, and that forcing them to allow those customers to leave their fortress walls could leave them vulnerable to the bandits who roam the land. They argue that users might be tricked into installing malicious software, or just badly written software that might be exploited to their detriment.

This is all true, but it's incomplete. Feudal warlords don't protect us out of a sense of patrician duty. The protection they extend is purely selfish: they protect us to the extent that doing so helps them maximize the revenues they earn from us. They will only protect us when other people threaten us: when they themselves are the threat, either due to a desire to harm us, or an indifference to putting us in harm's way, or because the profits from hurting us outstrip the profits from guarding us, their walled gardens become traps.

There are bad actors out there, roaming the land, but there are also bad actors right here, inside the app store. How can we protect ourselves? I'll get to that in the next chapter, right after we work through two more scenarios.

Getting the Message

Chances are, you have multiple messaging tools on your desktop or phone's home screen: Apple's iMessage, Facebook Messenger, WhatsApp, Google Chat, Signal and Telegram, along with the SMS app that interfaces with your phone company's texting service, an ancient protocol with its roots in the earliest flip-phones.

These messenger apps are well and truly driven by network effects: if your cousins abroad all use WhatsApp and you use Signal, either you have to convince them to install Signal, or they have to convince you to install WhatsApp. Every time you install a new network app, it tries to access your address book and alert existing users that you've signed up, but it doesn't do any such thing when you leave. The messenger companies know that the fact of your departure is bad news for their overall numbers, as it might prompt others to follow you.

The network effects on messenger apps are so strong that they have been the most dynamic technologies, rising and falling with enormous velocity, and battling fiercely among one another: there were the AIM/ICQ wars (settled when regulators permitted AOL to buy ICQ), the AIM/MSN wars, and then the wars with and among all the successors, Facebook Messenger, iMessage, Signal,

Telegram and all the many, many, many Google chat products, which the company fields and then shuts down every couple of years.

But throughout these forever wars, there have always been those who sued for peace. In 1998, a university student called Mark Spencer released a tool called Gaim that would allow Linux users to interconnect with the AOL Instant Messenger (AIM) network. It was an unofficial, third-party AIM client, produced without help from AOL—an example of adversarial interoperability.

AOL threatened trademark action against Gaim, over its incorporation of the letters "aim" in its name. In 2007, the project changed its name to "Pidgin." By then, Pidgin had progressed in sophistication and ambition, incorporating many different chat protocols and tying them all together.

If you had an account on Yahoo Messenger, AIM and Skype, Pidgin could let you manage them all from one app, sending messages to your friends no matter where they lived. Pidgin also had its own, super-secure messaging protocol, one of the first to use "end-to-end encryption"—meaning that messages were encrypted at one user's end and not decrypted until they reached the other end, meaning that no one in the middle could also read them.

Pidgin incorporated other interoperability tools, like XMPP, which MSN and Yahoo had once embraced in a bid to fight off the rising dominance of Skype (Microsoft later won that fight more definitively by buying Skype). It also expanded beyond Linux, becoming a kind of universal translator between all services and platforms.

But the commercial services abandoned XMPP and took steps to exclude Pidgin, preferring to fight for a winner-take-all network that they owned *in toto*. Today, Pidgin is maintained by a single developer, Gary Kramlich, who quit a lucrative job in tech and moved to a small town where he could live off of his savings while he devoted himself to the project. Kramlich supports millions of users this way. He understands that online messaging is at the heart of real, meaningful social interactions, online and offline, and that giving a single company control over that puts your ability to participate in family, work, romance and social life at their mercy.

In the fall of 2022, a reporter asked Apple CEO Tim Cook why he, the reporter, couldn't use all the features of Apple's messaging client with the reporter's mother, who uses an Android phone. Cook's answer? "Buy your mom an iPhone."

Recall the earlier discussion of "Turing Complete Universal von Neumann Machines" and universal computing. Every program that can run on an Android phone can run on an Apple phone—the reason the reporter's mother can't run a version of iMessage that does everything the iPhone version does is that Apple won't let her. Apple won't let her because Tim Cook thinks that might prompt her son to buy her an iPhone.

It's not exactly subtle.

Messaging has come a long way since the MSN/Yahoo/AIM wars. The most significant change is also largely invisible: today, nearly every major messaging tool incorporates the end-to-end encryption (E2EE) that Pidgin pioneered. The chat companies were slow to add this, and they proceeded in fits and starts, with many foolish missteps.

For example, Apple trumpeted the E2EE in iMessage but neglected to mention that iPhones default to making cloud backups of everything on your phone, including your stored messages, and this cloud backup isn't always E2EE—meaning Apple can snoop around in your messages in the cloud, as can cops who serve Apple with a warrant, hackers who compromise Apple's security or your account, and rogue Apple employees and their confederates.

Notably, Apple's cloud backups in China are "backdoored" and are monitored by government officials.

Message security is a high-stakes business. Some of the world's most notorious cyber-mercenaries—companies like the NSO Group—specialize in selling despots, dictators and torturers weapons to target messaging, and messaging attacks have been a prelude to all kinds of awful human rights abuses, including the Saudi government's murder and dismemberment of the journalist Jamal Khashoggi.

Gary Kramlich, the Pidgin maintainer, thinks about this a

lot. A cyber–arms dealer called Zerodium has posted a bounty of $100,000 for bugs in Kramlich's code, which they will turn into weapons that governments and powerful corporations can use to attack Kramlich's users. Recall that Kramlich works on Pidgin while living off his savings, and $100,000 would support four more years of that work. He jokes that he should deliberately insert a bug into his code, sell it to Zerodium, wait for the check to clear, then fix the bug. It's only a joke, though: Kramlich wouldn't deliberately expose his users to risk.

Closer to home, messaging attacks have targeted young women, famous and unknown, in order to steal intimate photos and videos intended for their own use or to share with a lover. These compromising images are used in blackmail, or uploaded to porn sites, or shared among their social circle, or published in tabloids.

To complicate things further, messaging security is a team sport, and your team is only as good as its weakest player. If you are engaged in a messaging dialog with a friend who has bad security practices—a weak password, say—then it doesn't really matter how secure your computer is, because your adversaries can target the person on the other end of the conversation instead.

This turns interop and messaging into a complex story: on the one hand, if you can send iMessages to your friends without using an iPhone (or using an iPhone, but with an app besides iMessage), then you can override the security weaknesses and compromises in Apple's own service. On the other hand, if you send an iMessage to a friend who has unwisely chosen an interoperable app that has security weaknesses, then your whole conversation might be exposed.

Any regulatory approach to interop in messaging has to be balanced between these two priorities. Unfortunately, regulators aren't handling this subject with the care it deserves. In 2022, the European Commission announced that the first phase of its Digital Markets Act—an interoperability mandate—would be to mandate interoperability for messaging tools—and that the whole thing had to be ready to go in two years.

This was a mistake. Two years isn't enough time to come up with a secure standard for federated messaging, let alone implement and test that standard (there are some existing standards, of course, but even if the EU simply orders the messaging companies to adopt them, there's still the need for very cautious and thorough testing of their implementations).

Other possibilities, like the use of "bridges"—which decrypt messages as they leave one network and re-encrypt them before sending them on to the next one—pose even greater risks. The same oppressive states and private cyber–arms dealers who focus their firepower on discovering and weaponizing bugs in existing systems would pour their efforts into compromising these bridges, as would criminals. That's because such bridges represent a prize more valuable than any "zero-day" (previously unknown) bug in any existing network, allowing attackers to spy on and disrupt *two or more* such networks.

This doesn't mean that bridges can't ever be used, or that individual users might not opt to run bridges on their own devices (imagine, say, an app that takes the messages that come in for you on Signal and displays them in your WhatsApp or vice versa, without ever sending these messages off your phone). But this arrangement wouldn't comply with the EU's Digital Markets Act, and it would still make users vulnerable to the whims of messaging companies themselves, whose arbitrary decisions to terminate their accounts could cut them off from family, friends, community and customers.

Beyond the immediate risks of a rushed interoperability mandate for messaging, there's also an important secondary risk from a botched job: a risk to the very idea of interoperability itself. If the first outing for the Digital Markets Act results in a privacy disaster that sees leaked sensitive messages, authoritarian violence, or fraud and identity theft (or all of the above), then every tech giant, of every type, will use that failure to attack interoperability and the DMA, insisting that lawmakers and regulators are just too darned clueless to regulate digital technology.

That's a common refrain, and it's made all the more credible by decades of idiotic tech policies, including those that create and protect tech monopolies, like anti-circumvention laws and other contributors to felony contempt of business model.

But it's an objection that should be framed as a question, not a statement: instead of stating "regulators are too clueless to regulate tech," we should be asking "*why* are regulators so clueless when it comes to regulating tech?"

After all, our world is *full* of high-stakes, highly technical regulatory questions that lawmakers manage to get right more often than they get wrong, despite lacking the direct experience needed to parse the issues themselves. Water purification, structural engineering, automotive and aviation safety, pedagogy and public education—the list goes on and on. The fact that you can drink your tap water safely despite the absence of any water chemists or microbiologists or public health specialists in Congress, Parliament or your state legislature means that lawmakers don't have to be experts in the issues that they pass laws about.

How can this be? They use experts: regulators are sometimes called "expert agencies," and their job is to solicit comment from other experts about the best rules for a given technical subject.

This process is grounded in the same premise as the scientific method: that the most reliable way to get at the truth is to have peers review one another's scientific claims, overseen by neutral expert referees whose job is to measure the quality of claims and counterclaims.

That's clearly something we *can* do with regulation, but it's something we no longer do in many areas—specifically, that adversarial, neutrally adjudicated process almost never applies to the regulation of monopolies and monopolistic cartels.

Those companies don't compete—that's the point. While the ad-tech duopoly—Facebook and Google—publicly claim to be fighting each other for your business, an antitrust investigation launched by dozens of US state attorneys general uncovered the existence of Jedi Blue, a secret, illegal pact between Google and Facebook to rig the ad market, dividing it up between themselves, misappropriating money that would otherwise go to publishers and making it impossible for competitors to offer a better deal.

When regulators seek comment on the best way to regulate ad-tech, they don't hear from a hundred small- and medium-sized companies, each with their own unique business model, each dedicated to highlighting the flaws in the others' argument. Instead, they hear from two giant companies with a combined market share of more than 80 percent, and then a bunch of pipsqueaks who are barely eking out a profit (often by being even *sleazier* than Google and Facebook!), as well as a bunch of academics and public interest types who don't work in the industry and are dismissed as being uninformed about its internal operations.

When lawmakers seek to regulate ad-tech, the floodgates open: the ad-tech duopoly have vast reserves of cash (because cartels are hugely profitable, thanks to the lack of margin-eroding competition) and they can easily decide how to spend it. They don't have to get a hundred fiercely competing companies to agree on a common lobbying position.

Regulators can't regulate tech because they're clueless, sure. But why are they clueless? Because the process by which regulators and lawmakers understand issues starts from the presumption that there will be an adversarial process and a neutral referee, and monopolies turn that into a chummy backroom deal between a handful of executives from the industry and a handful of their former colleagues who are temporarily regulating their former colleagues.

All of this is not to say that regulation should solely be the province of experts. Good regulation is the intersection of politics and expertise. *What* we want to do is a political question. *How* we do it is a technical question.

For example, in 2007, the psychopharmacologist David Nutt— then the "Drugs Czar" to the UK government—was asked to review the country's drug regulations, revisiting which substances were banned outright, which ones were available to some or all people and which ones required a doctor's prescription.

Nutt convened an expert panel that assigned three numerical scores to each drug, based on how dangerous those drugs were to the people who took them, to their families, and to wider society. These scores were aggregated, and, as expected, it became clear that some drugs were relatively benign to all three groups, while others were quite dangerous to all three groups.

But there was a third category of drugs: drugs whose danger rating changed drastically based on how the three priorities— harm to self, to family and to society—were weighted.

Nutt took his findings to Parliament, saying, effectively: "This group of drugs is benign and should be lightly regulated or exempt from regulation altogether. This second group of drugs is very dangerous and should be tightly regulated. How you regulate the third group of drugs depends on the relative importance you assign to these three different groups. There is no empirical answer to the question, 'Which matters more: self, family or society?' That is a *political* question, not a technical one. Once you have that answer, though, I can give you the *empirical* answer to your political directive."

This is how expert regulation and politics intersect.

Nutt was fired shortly thereafter. He refused to retract a scientifically grounded paper that demonstrated that cannabis was significantly less dangerous than alcohol. This caused the alcohol industry—dominated by a beer duopoly and a spirits duopoly—to erupt in outrage.

This handful of companies had hated Nutt from the start, when he ran an experiment that compared their self-regulated anti–binge-drinking curriculum to one of his own design, and showed that the reason the drinks cartel's anti-binge programs had failed was that they were very bad. Meanwhile, the drinks companies' own shareholder disclosures admitted that without binge drinking, they wouldn't turn a profit. But publicly they claimed to be working to end binge drinking and insisted that their failure to do so was due to the intrinsic difficulty of this project.

The booze merchants used his unwillingness to withdraw his evidence-based research findings to fire Nutt, something they had long wanted to do. The "Nutt sack affair" briefly dominated headlines and was then forgotten.

The Nutt sack affair is a perfect example of how regulation can go right—and wrong. It shows how expert, empirical findings feed into political choices, *and* it shows how monopolies can mobilize their profits, converting them into political power and using that to block good policymaking in favor of policies that help their shareholders and hurt the public.

It's inarguable that politicians around the world have struggled to make good tech policy, but this isn't down to some innate techno-cluelessness among the political classes. For the tech industry, the inability of politicians to make good policy is a feature, not a bug. When lawmakers pass impossible-to-follow regulations, these implode under the weight of their own contradictions, bolstering the tech industry's talking point that "politicians don't understand computers."

Meanwhile, the ongoing crises of badly regulated tech create the political will to *do something*, and the tech industry can intervene to make sure that that *something* is good for them and their shareholders.

We need to regulate tech. We need to regulate it well. We need to create regulations that are grounded in a nuanced, technical understanding of what is—and isn't—possible. We won't fix anything by demanding the impossible and shouting "nerd harder!" when tech companies fail to produce it. Nor will we fix anything by taking the tech industry at its word when it tells us that effective policies are flat-out impossible.

Progress depends on competence, political will, and vision. We need all three.

8

Jam Today:
How We'll Get There

In 2022, the EU passed the Digital Markets Act (DMA), mandating interoperability between Big Tech services and upstarts (what competition regulators call "new market entrants"): co-ops, startups, nonprofits and other alternatives. In the USA, the ACCESS Act has been introduced in two consecutive legislative sessions and at one point looked set to pass in 2022, though now that's looking less likely, for reasons unrelated to interoperability (2022 was the weirdest year yet in US congressional politics and a lot of the legislative calendar got turned over to culture war nonsense and hearings about the January 6th riots). In China, the Cyberspace Regulation forbids tech companies from blocking interoperability. The Canadian and British parliaments have both taken up interop as a remedy for monopoly.

But as I described in the previous section, it's hard to administer an interoperability mandate. Big companies will have every incentive to cheat and block interop, but also they will be *required* to effect these shutdowns when they detect attempts to attack their users with the interoperability interfaces mandated under laws like the DMA and the ACCESS Act.

In the previous chapter, I laid out a way to use mandates and comcom to corral companies into doing the right thing. Companies that cheat on interop laws are betting that cheating will make them more money than it costs them. It's a bet that sabotaging interop will scare off these "new market entrants" and train both customers and investors not to bet on them.

The penalties for cheating on the DMA or ACCESS Act will follow a long time after the cheating itself and might thus be the problem of future executives and managers, assuming they land after the execs who make the call to cheat jump ship for another company. But when those penalties *do* land, they can be whittled down in court—big companies can often trade lawyers' fees for fines at favorable exchange rates.

However, putting comcom in the mix changes this risk-reward calculus, and also creates a backup plan: if (when) the tech companies cheat on their obligations under an interop mandate, comcom lets those "new market entrants" continue to provide service. So if Apple blocks a third-party app store, legal comcom means that the blocked app store can supply its customers with jailbreaking tools so they can use its apps without Apple's cooperation. If Facebook blocks an interoperable online community, comcom means that their users can continue to communicate with their friends on Facebook using bots, scraping and reverse engineering.

All that sounds pretty abstract, so let me give you a concrete example of how an interop mandate went wrong, and how comcom might have saved it.

In 2012, when Massachusetts voters went to the polls, they got to vote on an automotive right-to-repair (R2R) ballot initiative. Normally, participation in these ballot initiatives is very low, but record numbers of Bay Staters who marked their ballot papers in 2012 weighed in on the R2R question. All told, 80 percent of them voted in favor of automotive R2R, which would force the auto manufacturers to share access to diagnostic information with independent mechanics, so any certified mechanic could fix your car. You wouldn't be locked into taking it to the manufacturer.

The state legislature duly enacted a R2R bill along the lines of the ballot initiative, but left a curious loophole. Under the law, automakers were required to give mechanics access to diagnostic information on their cars' internal *wired* networks.

The automakers promptly retooled and started sending diagnostic information over their vehicles' *wireless* networks.

For the next eight years, automotive right to repair in

Massachusetts steadily declined, as the proportion of cars that used wireless diagnostics increased.

But in 2020, another initiative appeared on the ballot—it replicated the measures in the 2012 proposal, but added wireless networks to the mandate. Once again, it carried by about 80 percent of the vote.

The people of Massachusetts were pretty adamant: they wanted to choose their own mechanics. They were steadfast in this determination, despite the automakers' attempts to scare the pants off of them. The big car companies flooded the airwaves with ads warning that their cars gathered so much intimate, compromising data on their drivers that allowing third parties to gain access to this data would expose car owners to *fatal* risk—one ad featured a woman being stalked through an underground parking garage by a shadowy figure who seems bent on nothing less than *murder.*

Of course, the obvious rejoinder to "Our cars spy on you so comprehensively that the data they extract could be used to plan your murder" is "How about if your cars stop spying on us, then?"

The new Massachusetts R2R rule is—as of this writing—still not in effect. The carmakers have so much ready cash (much of it accumulated by gouging drivers on maintenance) that they've been able to pay an army of lawyers to challenge the law in court.

It's the end of 2022. In the decade since Massachusetts voters went to the polls to affirm their overwhelming support for automotive right to repair, the actual state of right to repair in Massachusetts has been in free fall, as an ever-growing proportion of the cars on the road are becoming inaccessible to independent mechanics.

The mechanics were the first casualties of this attack. Drivers who brought their cars in for repairs would have to be turned away, because the local independent mechanic just couldn't diagnose their cars. Independent mechanics closed down their shops and exited the trade—or went to work for dealerships, who had a buyer's market for their labor and could name their prices and terms.

Drivers were the second casualty: there was no official list of all the cars that independent mechanics could fix. If you crossed your fingers and went to the local mechanic you'd used for years, there was a chance they could fix your car, but there was a growing probability that they'd get it up on the lift and tell you they couldn't even attempt the repair, and send you to the dealership.

Creditors and investors were the third casualty: mechanics struggled to service their bank loans or pay back the investors who'd taken a chance on their business.

Mechanics learned not to try to buck the system. Drivers learned not to try to go around the dealership's monopoly. The banks and investors learned never to bet against Big Car.

It's been a decade, and this is still the situation.

It didn't have to be that way.

Imagine a contrafactual with me for a moment. Imagine if comcom was on the scene. Imagine if three smart MIT kids could have reverse engineered those automotive diagnostic codes and designed a gadget with a $7 bill of materials, commissioned a factory in Guangzhou or Shenzhen to make a couple container-loads of them, then shipped them to the port of Los Angeles and trucked them to Cambridge, Massachusetts.

These little dongles could be sold to every mechanic in the state at $100 a throw. Not just in the state, either—every mechanic in America, in the *world*, has a use for such a gadget.

With margins like that, it's not hard to imagine that there would be investors interested in backing our trio—and helping them establish ancillary businesses, like third-party parts distribution, warranties and other high-margin services that strike at the core of the automakers' own commercial ambitions.

Perhaps just the threat of such a countermove would be sufficient to convince automakers to color within the lines and offer a managed, predictable third-party diagnostic tool offering that might erode their margins, but at least on their own terms.

But if it didn't, well, then, we'd still have the gadget. Mechanics could diagnose cars, so drivers could patronize the mechanics of their choosing. Everybody would win (except the automakers, who would lose, but honestly, fuck them).

That's what I mean when I talk about combining comcom and mandates to create something more powerful than either on their own. Mandates and comcom are like two-part epoxy: the mandate is strong, but brittle; comcom is flexible, but requires constant maintenance to keep it from bending out of shape. Together, they are strong *and* resilient.

Comcom was once the order of the day. Originally, there was no copyright on software at all. Then it acquired a "thin" copyright that could only be narrowly applied. Then, software acquired a copyright far beyond any ever applied to literary works, musical compositions, sound recordings, photos or moving images.

The prohibition on circumventing digital rights management, or DRM—embodied in Section 1201 of the DMCA, Article 6 of the EUCD and similar laws around the world—makes software the *most* copyrighted class of works in the world. Software authors (or rather, the corporations that employ them) enjoy more restrictions under copyright than the most talented composer, the most brilliant sculptor or the greatest writer.

But anti-circumvention is just the beginning. The thicket that blocks comcom is woven out of software patents, exotic contract theories ("tortious interference") and trademark, trade-secrecy, noncompete, nondisclosure and cybersecurity law, as well as other laws, policies and regulations. The thicket took decades to grow. Dismantling it is the work of decades. It's unlikely that a single omnibus bill modifying *all* of these laws could pass any legislature. It would gore far too many oxen. Even if it did, the court challenges could tie up the process for years or decades.

Not that we shouldn't try! We should! There are lots of long-term projects that deserve our commitment and attention (think: remediating climate change). But it's not enough to pledge ourselves to long-term reform—we need action *today*.

How can we get comcom back while we're waiting for decades of legislative reform to run its course? Here are three scenarios, in order of likelihood:

Binding Covenants

Companies sometimes agree not to block interoperability. For example, if your company wants to help create web standards at the World Wide Web Consortium (W3C), it has to promise not to enforce its patents against interoperators who implement the standards it helps create.

There are plenty of clubs that companies would like to join, where we can make comcom nonaggression pacts a condition of entry. Standards bodies can—and should—adopt a rule that says that members who join must make a legally binding promise not to invoke their rights under patents, copyright, anti-circumvention, trade secrecy, etc., against rivals who reverse engineer and extend their standards-compliant products, so long as this is done in service to privacy, security, usability, accessibility or competition.

But there's a much bigger, more important club that every large company *must* be a member of: the club of companies that supply government agencies and departments.

Governments all have "procurement rules" that define the minimum standards of conduct from the suppliers that sell goods and services to them: they specify what kind of insurance these companies must carry, how they must handle private data, how they must treat their workforce, where they must manufacture their products and source their inputs from, and so on.

Governments can—and should—have rules about interoperability in their procurement policies. They should *require* companies hoping to receive public money to supply the schematics, error codes, keys and other technical matter needed to maintain and improve the things they sell and provide to our public institutions.

That's not a radical proposition, it's just sound governance. Governments should spend public funds in ways that deliver value for money, and vendor lock-in does *not* deliver value for money.

The whole point of vendor lock-in is to give customers a stark choice: pay whatever the manufacturer is charging for software, parts, consumables and service, or throw the product away and start again. Maybe *you* can't make HP give up its ink-gouging grift, but if the US government announced that no federal department could buy a printer unless it accepted third-party ink, either HP would cave, or one of its rivals would.

This has a long and honorable tradition. When Abraham Lincoln sourced rifles for the Union Army, he insisted that they use interoperable tooling and ammo. I mean, *obviously*, right? "Sorry boys, no fighting today, the bullet factory took the week off. I'll tell the enemy and we'll meet back here tomorrow."

Amazingly, this is a lesson that even the US Department of Defense, the largest employer in America and an eight bazillion-pound gorilla in the procurements department, has forgotten. The US armed forces have long permitted themselves to buy materiel with single-source components—that is, parts that are made only by a single vendor.

Shrewd private equity investors noticed this and quietly gobbled up all these single-source suppliers (remember, the antitrust principle that competitors shouldn't be allowed to merge is essentially a dead letter). Then, these conglomerates *lowered* the price of their single-source parts (remember, the consumer welfare theory of antitrust says that pretty much anything goes, so long as prices go down).

These parts are now available below cost, which means that the primary military aerospace contractors (a handful of companies, thanks to an orgy of mergers) preferentially use these parts, filling aircraft, drones and other systems with parts that can only be purchased from a single supplier.

You might have predicted the next phase of the scam. While these parts are sold well below cost to the companies that *build* military jets, when the military needs to order those parts to *fix* those jets, the parts come with multi-thousand-percent markups. So long as the cost of fixing a jet is lower than the cost of replacing it, the military will pay.

Now, I happen to be a military abolitionist, but even so, I can't see any reason that military procurements should line the pockets of private equity profiteers who have figured out how to worm their monopoly products into the military's supply chain.

That goes double for all the *peacetime* public spending: government motor pools buying cars; school districts running Google Classroom; and administrative agencies buying Office365, Slack and Zoom licenses—they should extract binding promises from every one of these vendors not to attack interoperators who reverse engineer, modify and improve their products on behalf of government customers.

If every vendor selling to any branch of local, state or federal government has a binding nonaggression contract against adversarial interoperators, that opens whole swaths of products and services to reverse engineering and improvement.

Once a car is in a government motor pool, anyone can figure out how to bypass its VIN locks, provided they are doing so for a government customer.

The automakers will complain that there is no way that a diagnostic tool could be made readily available to every local, state and federal government agency without that tool leaking out into the hands of private-sector mechanics. They'll point out that private-sector mechanics sometimes fix public-sector vehicles, and so they'd be entitled to purchase and use these tools for their government customers, but it would be impossible to stop them from using those same tools on the privately owned cars that their other customers bring in for maintenance.

That is all 100 percent accurate.

So what?

It's not the government's job to figure out how to protect automakers' cockamamie repair-rigging schemes. It's the government's job to prudently administer public finances and public procurements. If automakers can't bear the emotional (or financial) strain of knowing that their customers have the option to entrust their car repairs to someone other than their authorized service depots, then those automakers can find a less emotionally taxing trade to pursue. Or they can just forego all public customers and take massive losses—some other automaker will choose to deal on terms in accord with good public procurement policy.

But they're right. If governments demand that companies promise not to sue or harass interoperators doing comcom on behalf of public-sector agencies, it will create a vast pool of comcom tools out there that will inevitably leak into all our hands.

State Limits on Contract

One-sided, bullying contracts are a major impediment to comcom. Companies use nondisclosure, noncompete, trade-secrecy, terms-of-service and "tortious interference" claims to prevent their competitors from offering interoperable products and services. They argue that these rivals can't even begin to reverse engineer their products without first "agreeing" to a contract in the form of a clickthrough or shrinkwrap license.

Then they argue that even if someone somehow *does* manage to reverse engineer their products without being trapped by one of these "agreements," that any comcom tool they provide to the public is "tortious interference." Translation: any customer who uses a comcom tool has already "agreed" not to do so when they clicked "I Agree" at the bottom of some endlessly scrolling garbage-novella of legalese. Under the "tortious interference" theory, the interoperator is in the wrong because they're abetting those customers to break *their* "agreements" with the original company.

Contract law is mostly regulated by states, and every state has its own set of contractual terms that are considered unenforceable; some states even ban certain terms from *appearing* in contracts.

Take California. The California state constitution makes non-compete agreements unenforceable. That turned out to be hugely important to the history of the state.

The first semiconductor company in California was founded by Robert Shockley, who won a Nobel Prize for figuring out how to make transistors out of silicon rather than gallium arsenide (which is why there's no Gallium Arsenide Valley). Shockley Semiconductor opened for business in 1955, and closed in 1968. It never had a successful microchip.

That's because Robert Shockley was a Nazi.

Shockley was an ardent eugenicist who devoted his energy to touring America and offering Black women shares of his Nobel prize money if they would promise to be sterilized and thus removed from the gene pool. He was a brooding, paranoid, hateful man, prone to wiretapping his employees and even his family, and that was a big reason why Shockley Semiconductor struggled to develop any sort of high-tech products, much less bring them to market.

Working for Robert Shockley was no fun. But because California banned noncompetes, eight of Shockley's top engineers ("The Treacherous Eight," in tech lore) were free to quit their terrible jobs, raise investment capital and start Fairchild Semiconductor, the first successful microchip company in Silicon Valley.

Fairchild was a nerd's playground—at first. But as time went by, the company ossified, coming under the sway of a straitlaced management committee, prompting two of the company's top engineers to quit and start their own company. They swiftly devastated the ranks of Fairchild, poaching the cream of their former colleagues to come work for them at their startup, which they called Intel.

Contract law is a powerful lever for encouraging—or starving—competition. California's policy of blocking noncompetes gave us Silicon Valley. Across the continent, Massachusetts's tolerance for noncompetes left the state's once-promising tech sector in California's dust. Neither Massachusetts nor California had a monopoly on companies founded by bad people with good ideas—but if you were unfortunate enough to join one of those companies in Massachusetts, you were stuck working for them. If you quit, you had to leave your chosen field for *three years* until your noncompete expired. Massachusetts startups became a place where good ideas went to die, dragging skilled technologists behind them.

When modern companies seek to block comcom, contract law is a powerful weapon. Terms of service can be invoked to ban users from availing themselves of interoperable tools (from third-party ink to third-party parts to ad blockers for social media), which also opens the door to tortious interference claims against the companies who make comcom tools.

Noncompetes can be invoked (outside of California) to prevent former employees from striking out on their own with interoperable products that help their previous employers' customers pay less and get more from the services they use. Trade secrets and nondisclosure can be invoked even when no noncompete exists, as a means of preventing former employees from directly competing with interoperable products and services.

All of these can be moderated by state-level rules on contracting; simply by banning certain terms, or declaring them unenforceable, states could kick open the doors to Big Tech's biggest silos. What's more, given the concentration of tech in a few geographic regions in the United States (and the problems associated with moving elsewhere), changes in just a few states could make a huge difference for people across America, and the world. Pass bills in California, New York and Washington and you'd be most of the way there. Throw in Texas and Massachusetts and you'd have nearly every base covered.

These changes would be good for business! Admittedly, they'd be bad for *giant*, stagnant monopolists, but they'd be good for all the small businesses that would nibble them to death with a thousand comcom products that shifted value back to users and workers, away from big institutional shareholders.

Adult Supervision

Earlier, I talked about the pending US ACCESS Act and the successful EU Digital Markets Act, powerful legislation that would force the biggest tech companies to open up their silos by making available APIs (gateways for exchanging information with their competitors). This is meant to allow interop without the messiness and unreliability of comcom.

But while an API *sounds* like a reliable way for users who quit a platform to go on communicating with the people they left behind there, it has one major weakness: the API has to be run by the big company, and it is designed to erode that company's monopoly profits by directly enabling its competitors to eat its lunch by luring away its most valuable users.

This creates a powerful incentive for the tech companies to cheat—not least because there are so many hard-to-detect ways to do so. They could slow things down to a crawl and blame too much traffic. They could throw out a lot of spurious error messages and shake their heads in bewilderment. They could introduce random dropped messages, say, 3 percent of the overall traffic, which would make everything kind of suck but be hard to decisively identify.

The point is, they could cheat.

And the tech giants *cheat all the time*. They are pathologically incapable of *not* cheating. Whether it's privacy law, competition law, labor law, environmental law—you name it, they cheat on it.

But for our purposes, that irresistible impulse to cheat is a feature, not a bug, as the tech bros say. Because for all that the tech giants cheat, they also kind of suck at it. They keep getting caught cheating. Either a disgruntled employee blows the whistle, or the conspirators just get sloppy.

When a tech giant cheats on the ACCESS Act or the Digital Markets Act, and when it gets caught, it will have to pay a *very* large fine. These laws are designed to *hurt*.

Obviously, cheaters will throw lawyers at the problem. When the fine runs into the billions, it's rational to spend hundreds of millions on outside counsel to get it reduced.

One thing those lawyers will eventually do is offer a settlement: "Let's just resolve this like reasonable people, and spare everyone all that delay and court expense, shall we?"

Here's the settlement we should offer them: a *special master*. A special master is a court-appointed guardian who supervises the conduct of a company or individual as part of a court procedure or settlement.

This person would act as adult supervision for cheating tech companies. Before a tech giant could sue or threaten another company, the special master would have to sign off on it, to make sure that the lawsuit was about enforcing against a true infringement and not merely a way to prevent a competitor from doing some comcom to help the cheater's customers get more privacy, usability, accessibility or equity.

This is like having a corporate parole officer, someone who

has to approve any moves outside the usual routine. It's a very big step to take, but very big companies demand very big steps.

Once a company has adult supervision, would-be interoperators are on a much surer footing. They can reverse engineer, scrape and take other comcom measures and know that the tech giant they're nibbling away at can't bring the law to bear against them, provided that they can make a case to the special master that they're acting on behalf of the users. That's an assurance that technologists can bring to investors or crowdfunders or granting agencies, opening up space for startups, social enterprises, nonprofits and co-ops to provide interoperable services.

The Interoperator's Defense

This one is way out there, but I want to include it. The world's major economies are in plenty of political turmoil, after all, and you never know who's going to end up with a congressional or parliamentary majority and an appetite for bold action.

With the Interoperator's Defense, we take a legislative shortcut. Rather than reforming copyright, trademark, contract, patent, trade-secrecy, cybersecurity and other laws so they can't be used to obstruct comcom, we just create a legal *defense* against claims under these laws (and others).

Here's how that defense works: someone can still sue you for breaking one of these laws, but in the early stages of the trial, you can put forward the defense that you were engaged in interoperability that furthered user privacy, security, accessibility or other legitimate interests. If the judge decides that's what you were doing, then the case ends.

This means that companies still get their day in court. They can still use the law to shut down people who hack their service and hurt their users. But interoperators *also* get a day in court. They can use a relatively cheap, relatively fast legal process to get past otherwise punitively expensive and time-consuming courtroom fights with monopolists whose legal budgets are effectively unlimited—who might be willing to spend otherwise irrational sums of money getting the courts to put interopera-tors out of business because that will scare off future comcom upstarts.

Interop mandates and comcom are no substitutes for tradi-tional antitrust remedies like corporate breakups. There's just no fair way for massive, deep-pocketed companies to operate app stores and compete with the companies that sell apps in those stores; or sell ebooks and also compete with the authors and publishers who publish on their ebook stores; or serve search results and also compete with the companies listed in those results; or operate a social media network and also operate the *other* social media network that people leave for when they get pissed off with the first one.

But breakups take a *long-ass time*. If you look up the breakup of AT&T, you'll be told that it took seven years. That's an extremely misleading figure! In truth, US competition regula-tors first took on AT&T *sixty-nine* years before the company was broken up. For most of the intervening decades, AT&T was fending off some kind of attempt to tame it.

AT&T was allowed to secure a monopoly, and *then* regulators tried to bring it to heel. This is exceedingly difficult. Monopolies have very deep pockets (recall IBM outspending the US DoJ for twelve consecutive years during "antitrust's Vietnam"), and they can co-opt powerful stakeholders to cape for them when antitrust regulators bang on the door (AT&T was nearly broken up in the mid-fifties, but the Pentagon leapt to its defense, insisting that the United States would lose the Korean War if AT&T wasn't left unmolested).

We *have* monopolies, lots of them, in every sector, including tech. With monopolies, an ounce of prevention is worth a ton of cure. But, as the old Irish joke goes, "If you wanted to get there, I wouldn't start from here."

Tech's critics rightly decry "tech exceptionalism," the idea that tech is different and so should play by a different set of rules—think, for example, of Google and Facebook's claims that privacy-invading conduct that we wouldn't tolerate if they were carried out by flesh-and-blood people following us around the world should remain unchecked.

But there *are* at least two ways in which tech is exceptional:

First, tech is foundational. The questions of tech monopoly aren't *inherently* more important than, say, the climate emergency or gender and racial discrimination. But tech—free, fair, open tech—is a precondition for winning those other fights. Winning the fight for better tech won't solve those other problems, but *losing* the fight for better tech extinguishes any hope of winning those more important fights.

Second, tech is *interoperable*. That means that, long before we break up Facebook or Google or Microsoft or Apple, we can offer immediate, profound relief to the people whose freedom of motion is hemmed in by tech's walled gardens. We don't have to wait for breakups to allow someone to install a third-party app, or bypass heavy-handed (or overly tolerant) moderation, or overcome the algorithmic burial of their material. We can do that right now, with interop.

And when we do, we hasten breakups! The bullying that walled gardens enable isn't driven by sadism, after all, but by *profit*. Letting people wriggle out of companies' bad decisions means that those companies will lose the money they would have otherwise earned thereby—and if companies behave better to prevent those users from defecting, then they will forego the profits they would have realized by acting worse.

Monopolies need those profits to defend themselves from trustbusters. Hiring more lawyers than the DoJ isn't cheap, and IBM wouldn't have been able to pay those bills if it hadn't been piling up a war chest by abusing its monopoly for decades. Interop starves the beast, depriving monopolists of the excess profits they would otherwise be able to use to keep trustbusters at bay. With interop, it's harder for a company to make itself too big to jail.

But interop also makes it harder for a company to make itself too big to fail. The Pentagon wouldn't have been such an ardent defender of AT&T if it hadn't been so dependent on Ma Bell: if the US military could have easily uncoupled itself from AT&T— by buying interoperable products and services to replace the ones that Bell Labs supplied—then the Defense Department might have been less eager to go to war to defend the Bell System.

And, as President Lincoln knew, the military shouldn't be single-sourcing its key capacity to one company without at least securing a promise of interoperability.

Starve monopolies of the profits used to hold trustbusters at bay, cut them off from the allies who fight trustbusters on their behalf, and maybe it won't take sixty-nine years to break up Microsoft. Or Apple. Or Google. Or Facebook. Or Salesforce. Or Oracle.

PART II

What About

9

What about Privacy?

Feudal security works well. Right now, the Big Tech platforms employ an army of security experts—mercenaries who stand on the bristling battlements of their walled gardens, ready to fend off barbarians who would steal user data.

I speak against tech monopolies at many security conferences, and without fail, I'm confronted by an audience member—a skilled security practitioner—who wants me to know that the bad guys they do hand-to-hand combat with all day, every day, are unspeakable monsters, who will use whatever private information they can steal from tech platforms to torment innocent people in unspeakable ways.

They're absolutely correct. The depredations of identity thieves, stalkers and fraudsters are serious, even sometimes fatal (as when your leaked home address is used in a "SWATting" attack, where someone calls the police pretending to be you, feigning panic about an "active shooter" that matches your own description).

Tech bosses pay these security experts a lot of money to defend us all from these external threats. But one thing tech bosses will *never* pay security experts to do is defend us from the tech bosses themselves.

Feudal security *fails badly.* If a company decides to betray your trust and invade your privacy, the security experts won't defend you from their own employers—instead, they'll turn on interoperators who step in to defend you.

While I was writing this passage, I was contacted by the founders of a little startup called OG App. OG App is an "alternative Instagram client." Use it—instead of the official Instagram app—and you will get an "OG" Instagram feed: just the posts your friends have made, in the order that they made them, with no ads.

What's more, OG App doesn't do any of the fine-grained surveillance that the official Instagram app engages in. The official Instagram app sends a constant stream of "interaction telemetry" back to Meta—every tap, touch and scroll. The only time OG App sends data to Instagram is when *you* tell it to, by liking or commenting on a post.

If you're an Instagram user, you might be thinking about rushing off to get a copy of OG App for your Android device or iPhone, but you're out of luck. Just hours after OG App's launch, Apple yanked it from the App Store. A few days later, Google kicked it out of Google Play, the app store for Android. Then, Facebook's internal team tracked down the identities of OG App's founders and *permanently banned them* from Facebook.

Apple, Google and Facebook all tell stories about how they view "privacy" and "openness" (as I write these words, someone has sent me an article in which Mark Zuckerberg claimed to be an advocate of "open systems" in contrast to Apple's closed approach), and Apple has plastered every major city in the United States with billboards touting its commitment to privacy.

Back in 2008, Facebook sold itself as the privacy-friendly alternative to MySpace—and it was! Back then, Facebook wasn't interested in your private data. Then it changed its mind, and the fortress that Facebook used to keep data-miners *out* turned into a prison that locked its users *in*, where their data could be more readily plundered.

Companies *can* defend our privacy, and they often *do*, but when they choose not to—because they value something else more highly, or because they change corporate strategy—then you have no recourse but to leave. And where companies have used lock-in strategies to punish you for leaving, you might choose to give up your privacy rather than endure the switching costs they've engineered into the system.

Interoperability's superpower is reducing those switching costs, but interoperators might betray you in exactly the same way that Apple, Facebook and Google have (remember when Google's corporate motto was "Don't be evil"?).

The answer can't be to trust the big companies—and it can't be to trust the small companies, either.

Instead, the baseline for your privacy should be set by democratically accountable regulation. Privacy laws like Europe's General Data Protection Regulation set out a framework for informed, enthusiastic consent for collecting, storing and handling private data.

The GDPR has been plagued by weak enforcement, preferentially wielded against smaller firms who can't afford to fight back. It's true that many of these smaller firms are even sleazier than the big American tech companies, but that's not why European regulators targeted them—the regulators didn't have the resources to engage in long legal battles with tech giants, so they went after the little guys. Easy pickings.

When James Comey—now famous for his turn as head of the FBI through the 2016 Trump election—was made US attorney for the Southern District of New York, he gathered his prosecutors and asked who among them had never lost a case. When many of the lawyers proudly raised their hands, Comey called them "the Chickenshit Club." They had only ever turned their enforcement powers on villains who couldn't defend themselves, rather than prioritizing the worst offenders, whose ill-gotten gains provided them with the war chest they needed to exact huge resource costs from the State of New York if it tried to hold them to account.

There's a lot of Chickenshit Club in the enforcement history of the GDPR. US tech giants routinely flout its rules. Either they make data collection opt-out (under the GDPR, it must be opt-in), or they refuse service to users who opt out (also prohibited under the GDPR), or they claim they don't need your consent to take your data, because they have a "legitimate purpose" for doing so (the GDPR does indeed have a "legitimate purpose" carve-out for data processing without consent, but there's no reasonable case that the Big Tech companies are engaged in activities that it permits).

Despite this weak enforcement (and despite shoehorned, ill-starred clauses in the GDPR like the "right to be forgotten"), the core of the GDPR is solid. It says that online service providers may not capture, store or process your data without your enthusiastic, freely given consent.

Those are the rules that we should apply to *all* the people who interact with your personal information, whether they're a giant tech platform or a tiny interoperator that wants to exchange messages with giant tech platforms.

Enforcing a rule like the GDPR is hard—as the European experience shows. But as the American experience shows, there's no substitute for it. We can't rely on giant companies to always do the right thing—not even companies like Apple, who spend millions telling us all that they're privacy fanatics who'll take a bullet to protect our identities.

How do you keep enforcers from joining the Chickenshit Club? That's the rub, isn't it?

I'll tell you how *not* to do it: by preserving the giant tech companies intact on the grounds that they need to be more powerful than most governments if they are to muster the resources to defend our privacy. Any company more powerful than the government is a company the government won't be able to hold to account—that's the very definition of too big to jail.

If we want to have privacy online *all the time*—and not just when a techno-feudal warlord decides we deserve it—we *must* have some force other than companies to make the call about what conduct is and is not permissible. A democratically accountable force. A good regulator, enforcing a good regulation, who doesn't want to join the Chickenshit Club.

10

What about Harassment?

Harassment is a real problem online. It's not just a matter of snowflakes with hurt fee-fees: there are harassment gangs—some who work for corporations or causes or governments in order to stifle criticism, some simply organized around the sadistic pleasure of shouting down their ideological adversaries.

When they come at you on social media, filling your wall or your timeline with vicious insults, often cruelly personalized with references to your family members (for example, threats about your children, along with their names and photos, or disparaging remarks about recently deceased loved ones you've publicly grieved online), it is hard to endure.

Many people have been chased offline by trolls. And while anyone can find themselves targeted by an organized harassment campaign, the most frequent targets are women, particularly trans women and/or women of color. That is, harassers go after the people who are afforded the least respect and concern overall in our society.

Getting chased offline by trolls is no fun—and it certainly doesn't represent a triumph for "free speech"—a talisman often brandished by trolls, especially when they're ganging up on someone they disagree with in the hopes of silencing them.

It's hard to say what's worse, though: getting chased offline by trolls, or feeling like you *can't* leave an online space where you are subjected to a constant barrage of harassment. Why do people go to places where harassers are welcome? Why do they sometimes stay, even when the harassers make their lives a living hell?

Blame network effects. Think back to the introduction of this book: network effects are the forces that make products and services more valuable based on the number of people who use them. In the case of social media, the harassment targets who stick with platforms that make them miserable do so because the platforms have penned in the people that matter to them: the customers, communities and friends they want—need—to stay in contact with.

When a platform corrals everyone important to you, you're going to stay on that platform, even if the platform is badly run.

Now, we can and should ask the platforms to clean up their acts and do better about blocking harassment, but any platform with millions (let alone billions) of users is going to struggle to distinguish harassment from other activities (including complaining and commiserating about harassment, in which the language of harassers is repeated verbatim). If we can't harassment-proof the platforms, we can at least make them easier to leave. Interoperable social media, federated among servers that are responsible to their users, would let harassment targets leave the big platforms for smaller, more responsive ones, where habitual harassers—and the servers they use—could be blocked at the gate. And because those servers would remain connected to the big, incumbent systems like Facebook and Twitter, leaving them for somewhere less painful wouldn't mean leaving behind the people who matter to you and the pleasure they bring you.

11

What about Algorithmic Radicalization?

People believe some weird stuff these days. Before QAnon gobbled up the conspiratorial fringe, there was a thriving online "flat Earth" movement of people who were convinced the spherical Earth was a conspiracy involving NASA and innumerable other agencies who wanted to hide the fact that we were spinning through space on a domed saucer.

No, really.

QAnon, stolen elections, vaccine denial and all those other fringe notions have absolutely found their home online, and the internet has definitely helped them spread. But *why* is that?

Some people think it's because the big platforms are really good at "algorithmic persuasion." Somehow, platforms combine the data they nonconsensually acquire about your preferences and activities with some kind of algorithmic processing and out pops a way to present a proposition to you that just *slides* past your critical faculties and comes to rest lodged in your enduring belief systems.

If this is true, it's not just terrifying, it's *amazing*. People have been trying to come up with some kind of mind control for centuries, and every alleged success has been either a self-deception or just, you know, a deception. From Rasputin to MK-Ultra, from Mesmer to neuro-linguistic programming, every claim to mind control has turned out to be *bullshit*.

Which is not to say that there's no basis for a belief in the power of algorithmic persuasion. The ad-tech companies—Google and

Facebook—spend a lot of time boasting about how good they are at it. Of course they do! They're *advertising companies*. The one thing every successful advertising company is good at, by definition, is convincing advertisers that advertising works. But just because a latter-day digital Mad Man can convince a blue chip company to pay a premium for advertising services, it doesn't mean that the company will benefit from its purchase. When Procter & Gamble zeroed out its $100,000,000-a-year digital ad budget in 2017, it saw *no* change in sales.

One thing we know for certain about the Big Tech companies is that they lie all the time: they lie about which data they collect from you; they lie to advertisers about whether you saw an ad; they lie to publishers about whether they collected money for an ad. They lie about their taxes, their labor practices and every other commercially significant subject.

Wouldn't it be amazing if the only time they told the truth was when they boasted about how great their products are?

I don't think the tech companies invented a mind-control ray to sell your nephew a fidget spinner, only to be outsmarted by right-wing billionaires who hijacked it and used it to turn your uncle into a QAnon.

But if tech companies aren't facilitating mind control, what is going on with "online radicalization?"

It's complicated, but here's what I think is up.

First, "engagement-maximizing" algorithms do *something*, even if it's not mind control. Let's consider a more benign example to explain what I mean.

Say you go out shopping for kitchen cabinets, and for the first time you start thinking about joinery and finish carpentry; that is, how those sturdy, sharp corners in wooden cabinets are made.

You don't know those terms, though, so you go home and type "How are kitchen cabinets made" into Google and click a YouTube link like the one I just found, "How All-Wood Cabinets Are Made." It's a 2:44 vid from a cabinet-making service in Florida. It's pretty good, but more interesting is that it coughs up the term "joinery."

A search for "joinery" turns up an eight-minute video on Japanese joinery by an Instagram-famous Japanese carpenter.

It's a wordless, hypnotic video of nail-free joinery techniques. In the title of the video is the transliterated Japanese phrase "Kane Tsugi," a "three-way pinned corner mitre" joint. The video also helpfully provides some Japanese characters that I can search with: "面代留め差しほぞ接ぎ."

Searching for "面代留め差しほぞ接ぎ" yields up a banquet of videos on Japanese joinery, and from there, I learn about more kinds of Japanese joinery. One click later, I'm watching a thirty-minute NHK "Japanology" documentary about Sashimoto woodwork, of which "Kane Tsugi" is a subset. That gets me to a kind of tongue-and-groove joint called a "hashibame," but YouTube doesn't have anything else on that.

Instead, I go back to search engines, and from there, to Japanese search terms, and from there, to Google Translate versions of Japanese sites, including message boards where they're discussing the finer points of hashibame in detail.

This is a "radicalization" funnel. I started off not knowing much about a subject—not even what it was called! From there, I learned a few search terms, which got me channeled into a specific area (just as searches for "flat Earth evidence" and "flat Earth conspiracy" steer you into different online communities).

The engagement-maximizing algorithm has learned from those who came before me that many people can be lured into longer online sessions if they are presented with a list of specific subtopics branching off the general topic they've landed on. This isn't a unique or sophisticated insight: it's the organizing principle behind every kind of information organizing scheme. Dewey Decimal 600 is "Technology and Applied Sciences"; drill down a level to 690 for "Building"; another level takes you to 694, "Wood Construction." From there, you can add suffixes for "Japanese" and so on.

This isn't to dismiss hierarchical information organization as trivial—on the contrary, it's extremely powerful, which is why it recurs in so many places. The advent of digital libraries only increased this power, by allowing a single resource to be "filed" in multiple places (a physical book can only be on one shelf at a time; the same video can be linked from hundreds of places).

Thus digital systems make for extremely efficient paths between general, top-level subjects and specific, narrow, esoteric ones, even for users who don't know what they're looking for.

There's no question that this can lead you astray (as anyone who's ever tried to look up a sick headache on Google and come away half an hour later convinced they have a rare brain tumor can attest), but this is conceptually very different from the "algorithmic radicalization" narrative that has nefarious actors brainwashing hapless alternative-medicine enthusiasts and anti-authoritarians into becoming heavily armed anti-mask rioters.

Now, there's also no question that there are nefarious actors out there and that they benefit from digital systems, because our digital systems are designed to help find people with certain traits, especially rare ones. Obviously, this is key to targeted advertising, which lets you choose to show your ad for refrigerators to people who've been browsing kitchen renovation sites, or your ad for baby food subscriptions to people who've been reading up on prenatal health.

But the imperative for digital systems to locate people predates the rise of targeted advertising. The very earliest online social spaces—dial-up "Bulletin Board Systems" (BBSes), online services like CompuServe and Usenet, which ruled the internet in the pre-web years—organized on topical lines specifically so that people could find others to discuss subjects of interest with them.

From its earliest days, the internet has been a system for people with esoteric views to come together. This is a mixed blessing, to be sure, but that it is a blessing is hard to deny: the idea that "Black lives matter" was once a fringe view, as was the idea that gender is not a binary. Beyond politics, the infinite subdivision of the internet into interest-oriented spaces is great for discovering new science-fiction authors, techniques for making really shiny mudballs, and detailed notes on creating special-effects makeup, brewing beer, fixing cars, restoring old furniture or getting advice for nursing a sick tropical fish.

It's *also* great for finding Nazis to hang out with. It's great for finding transphobic stalkers to join forces with in order to harass trans people. It's great for finding people to flesh out and reinforce unhinged conspiracies about Jews controlling the world, or "elites" scheming to hide the fact that the Earth is flat.

The internet's capacity for interest-linked communities is especially important in light of the "echo chambers" that dominate our physical lives. The past forty years have seen an increased clustering by income, class, racial background and other coarse demographic features that are also reliable predictors of social views and attitudes. In our "real" lives, we are far *less* likely to meet people who (openly) espouse views that fly in the face of our local orthodoxy, or express identities that are unacceptable in our immediate physical communities.

This is one of the reasons that being online feels so "extreme"—if you don't live in a place where open racism is socially acceptable, it can feel like the internet is a swamp of people saying things at a digital remove that they would never say in person. While some people are certainly disinhibited by the distancing effect of online interactions, many of the "trolls" we meet online are exactly the same people they are offline. The difference is that their views are not considered as extreme by the people in their offline lives, and those people also know that old Bill (or Tom, or Fred or Bertha) is always running their mouth and is all bark and no bite.

But breaking out of your place-based filter bubbles and finding online communities where the norms are very different from those in your home and neighborhood can be a godsend. It's how queer kids in conservative Christian households find one another; it's how young feminists being raised by misogynists and atheists being raised by fundamentalists escape their surroundings. It's how people who find it impossible to believe that drought or wildfires are "normal" learn about the urgency of the climate emergency.

(It's also how you discover that you were born to play Dungeons & Dragons, or listen to Bulgarian folk music, or have a polyamorous marriage, or become an ardent bird-watcher; the internet lets us find out what kinds of people we are.)

The internet helps us find subjects we didn't know we were interested in; it lets us find people who are interested in those subjects. But the internet does one more thing: it lets us coordinate with those people to *do stuff*.

The internet lets swingers find sex parties. It lets Wikipedians find articles to edit. It lets adventurers find dungeon masters. It lets millions of Americans join a Women's March against Trump.

It lets Nazis converge on Charlottesville, Virginia.

The "online radicalization" question assumes that the problem is that the internet lets people who are susceptible to hatred and scapegoating and violent fantasies find one another, but it doesn't ask where those forces come from. "Online radicalization" assumes that the rise of monopolies, the looming climate emergency, crushing debt, soaring inequality and grinding austerity are *separate questions* from "Why are people so angry? Why are they looking for someone to blame? Why are they willing to turn to hatred and violence?"

"Online radicalization" insists that flat Eartherism and vaccine denial are phenomena unrelated to corrupt, captured regulatory agencies—that there is no connection to the regulatory malpractice that led to a million dead from the opioid epidemic, nor to the mistrust of pharma companies and the FDA that drives vaccine denial.

I don't know any way that we can prevent "extremists" from meeting up online and convincing one another that sexual, religious and racial minorities are to blame for their miseries—certainly not one that doesn't inflict far greater harm on sexual, religious and racial minorities.

But here's what I do know: "radicalization" is the *end* of a pipeline, and it is preceded not just by finding people who offer seductive and misleading solutions to real problems—it is preceded by the problems themselves.

Tech monopolies are *epiphenomena*: they are effects, not causes. They are the *effect* of an ideology that embraces monopolies and inequality as a natural, even inevitable phenomenon. It's an ideology that lionizes monopolists as once-in-a-generation geniuses who *deserve* the power to structure the daily routines and constraints of billions of their fellow humans.

That is the ideology that produces regulatory capture (because when an industry consists of a handful of companies, everyone qualified to regulate it is a veteran of one or more of its largest corporations). It's the ideology that convinces people that democratic institutions are no match for corporate power. It's a counsel of despair.

It's true that weakening the corporate power of Big Tech will also reduce its ability to police our online discussions for signs of "radicalization," but Big Tech has *never* been very good at this, has it? Meanwhile, weakening corporate power also weakens the case for conspiratorial beliefs that the official truth is what *they* want you to believe.

Speaking for myself, I'd rather have a world with no Big Tech to downrank and delete conspiratorial posts, if it meant that we'd have a world with no Big Tech to *inspire* those conspiratorial beliefs.

12

What about Child Sexual Abuse Material, Nonconsensual Pornography and Terrorist Materials?

There are plenty of odious ideas, images and files that you would rather never see—say, racist editorial cartoons, rambling defenses of homeopathy and conspiratorial views about whether humans ever visited the Moon. While you may prefer to inhabit conversational spaces in which these subjects are not raised, most reasonable people will grudgingly allow that other people are allowed to hold *unreasonable* views, and to discuss them amongst themselves. In other words, you might kick someone out of your living room for spouting racist bullshit, but you don't think that they should be prohibited from spouting the same bullshit in *their own* living room.

But there's some material that isn't just *awful* but *unlawful*—stuff that shouldn't exist, period. The go-to case here is child sex abuse material (CSAM), the current term of art for what many people call "child pornography."

But a moment's reflection will yield up lots of material beyond CSAM that most of us would like to see prohibited altogether and not merely barred from polite society. Nearly everyone would like to stop the spread of nonconsensual pornography (AKA "revenge porn"). Most of us would like to extinguish the trade in hacked personal information, such as financial information, but also including passwords, home addresses, medical records and other information of use to extortionists and identity thieves.

But then it starts to get complicated. There's a totally understandable, widespread horror of terrorist atrocity videos—but efforts to stamp these out have also resulted in the mass deletion of repositories of evidence of war crimes, painstakingly assembled and cataloged by survivors of those atrocities against the day they can be used to hold their tormentors to account in The Hague or at some other tribunal.

Replacing Facebook and other monoliths with interoperable, federated systems will spell the end of the era in which we outsource the enforcement of laws regarding unlawful speech to the big platforms.

That's because the goal here is to make it so those platforms have less power over us. Right now, if Facebook or Twitter or Reddit or Google blocks a piece of content, it effectively ceases to exist for billions of people.

That has led some of us to think of independent sites as "shadowy corners" of the internet: when hatemongers and conspiratorialists decamp to 8chan or Kiwi Farms in order to conduct conversations that are banned on the big platforms, we talk about the act of evading Big Tech moderation as being just as suspect as the conversations themselves.

These are not equivalent acts. The desire to have a discussion beyond the reach of moderators at Facebook, Twitter, Google and Reddit is perfectly legitimate.

What's less legitimate is carrying on a discussion promoting Holocaust denial, eugenics, "race science" or quack medical theories that lead to sick people risking their lives by refusing effective treatment. And trading nonconsensual pornography, child sex abuse material or materials stolen via identity theft is *illegitimate*—indeed, it's illegal.

It's important to maintain a distinction between "things that we wish people didn't say" and "things that are crimes." In the United States, Holocaust denial and quack eugenic theories are legal, even if they are widely viewed as odious. A federated social media world is one where we replace a single, centrally managed town square with a web of small social spaces—more akin to private kitchen tables or clubhouses or your local bar than a podium on the steps of the town courthouse.

Much as I don't want people to be Holocaust deniers, I also don't want anyone to tell me what I can discuss with people who've joined me in a private space.

Federated online spaces will offer more "dark corners" where these ideas can be aired without fear of censure or account deletion. But they will also allow more tools for people who don't want to associate with or hear from people with odious views.

Today, discussions of how federated social media will affect content moderation focus on people who want to say things that big social media companies won't let them say. What that discussion omits is that federated social media will also allow you to *block* things that big social media companies *permit*.

In other words, if you want to live in a world where no one ever tries to tell you that you can prevent Covid-19 with sunshine and vitamins, you can move to a server where that's the house rule—a server that only federates with other servers that share that house rule. People who sign up for servers where "alternative" medicine—or "race science" or climate denial or some other conspiratorial view—is permitted can talk to one another about it, but they can't talk to *you* about it. And remember, the point here is to reduce the power and centrality of big platforms, which means that you can't cook up a conspiracy in some fever swamp of your own and then game the algorithms of Big Tech platforms to put it front and center of millions of other people.

The internet doesn't make more people vulnerable to bad ideas, but it lets ideas of all kinds—bad and good—spread widely. It's as though we've all moved from the countryside, where we all got water from our own wells, into a city, where we all drink from a central reservoir. It was always possible that the drinking water for one family or small community would get a bad microbe in it and sicken the people who drank from it, but that sickness didn't keep spreading, because of the distance that isolated one group from the next.

Once everyone is cheek-by-jowl in a city, any sanitation problem affects everyone—because once your water is contaminated, you can go on to sicken others. Allowing online groups to establish some distance from one another—to cluster *and* to separate—re-establishes some of the distance that braked the spread of ideas before.

Call it an "echo chamber" if you like, but it's fairer to say "a home." We need public forums where ideas rub up against one another, and we also need quiet places where ideas can be floated and discussed among people of similar orientation. Online trolls have figured this out; they had to, because they got kicked off the big platforms. The rest of us shouldn't cede the idea of spaces run by and for their communities to 8chan trolls. It's not just the worst people in the world who benefit from semiprivate, autonomously operated homes whose membership is confined to people who broadly agree with you.

But this kind of separation *does* work against the dominant means of enforcing against *illegal* content. Facebook, Google, Apple and the other big platforms pour tremendous energy into detecting and blocking identity theft materials, CSAM and other outlaw content, as well as other content that is more contentious (copyright infringement, terrorist incitement, etc.).

Google, Facebook and Apple can only block the spread of this content to the extent that it is shared on Google, Facebook and Apple's systems. If a child sex abuse ring distributes its files using servers of its own, the transactions are invisible to Google, Facebook and Apple. What they can't see, they can't stop.

This is true, but I don't believe it militates for forcing all content to touch a server owned by a Big Tech platform so that it can be logged, examined and, if necessary, reported to law enforcement.

Why not? Well, for starters, Google, Facebook and Apple aren't democratically accountable public institutions—they are privately held, shareholder-value-maximizing firms. For all that they interdict harmful activities, they also enable a host of them, including the harms of surveillance, which is an invaluable aid to autocratic governments, stalkers, identity thieves and other abusers and crooks. Law enforcement shouldn't be a function of private corporations, especially not *these* corporations.

First, because even if they can do it, they shouldn't. Turning

Big Tech into an integral part of our public safety apparatus may seem convenient, but it also means that we can't cut Big Tech down to size without endangering public safety. It's a devil's bargain. Remember how AT&T avoided a breakup in 1956 because the Pentagon stepped in to insist that America would lose the Korean War if AT&T wasn't there to help in the fight?

But then there's the fact that Big Tech *isn't* good at this.

Facebook maintains a terrorist watchlist that it distributes to other tech platforms—a list of people who shouldn't be allowed on the internet because they're trying to recruit other terrorists and generally spread terror.

At the time of this writing, Facebook is being sued by a group of sex workers who allege that Facebook's top executives took bribes from OnlyFans to add these sex workers to the terrorist watchlist. The performers had quit OnlyFans and struck out for platforms that treated them better and paid them more, and OnlyFans, the suit alleges, wanted to make sure they failed on these new platforms, lest their success tempt other performers to quit the service.

It's not that public officials running a terrorist watchlist couldn't use it in vindictive or corrupt ways. Terrorist watchlists are bullshit. They are sprawling, out-of-control blacklists that should be abolished. Maybe we will abolish them, if we can hold our governments to account.

But Facebook's terrorist watchlist *can't* be held to public account, because Facebook isn't a public institution, and its watchlist is a private, self-regulated initiative that its competitors have voluntarily signed up for. It is a shadow court, a star chamber, and it's run by people with a track record of abusing their power (one of the executives accused of personally accepting bribes is Nick Clegg, the former deputy prime minister of the United Kingdom).

Google operates a CSAM filter for its cloud services. When users upload images to Google Photos, an automated filter evaluates those images to determine whether they might be CSAM, and if it thinks you're trafficking in child pornography, it notifies a human Googler, who can then notify the police. That's what happened to "Mark," except Mark *wasn't* trafficking in abuse images—he was the father of a toddler with an infected penis. His son's pediatrician asked Mark to submit a photo of his son's infection using the medical practice's secure portal.

However, Mark's phone was also set up to synchronize his photos with Google Photos, via the cloud. When he took a picture of his son's penis, that picture automatically uploaded to Google's cloud, and Google's machine-learning child porn detector flagged it to human beings at Google, who turned Mark over to the San Francisco Police Department, along with Mark's entire search history, his email and all the other data Google had collected on him.

To the SFPD's credit, they swiftly concluded that Mark wasn't a child pornographer, just a dad with a sick kid who forgot to uncheck the "auto-upload" button while trying to follow his doctor's instructions.

Not Google.

Google deleted his account and all his data, including every family photo he'd ever taken. He lost his phone number (he was a Google Fi customer). He lost his phone, too (he was an Android user). He lost his email address. He lost the two-factor authentication he used to log in to accounts, which meant that he lost every other account that relied on either 2FA, a phone number or email to log in. He lost every document he had on Google's cloud.

Which is to say, he lost everything. Indeed, he was so thoroughly cut off by Google that the SFPD detective who contacted him to tell him that he wasn't a suspect and everything was fine had to do so by postal mail, because he couldn't call or email.

Google says they won't give Mark his account back because they found another "problematic" image in his files, "a young child lying in bed with an unclothed woman." Mark says he doesn't know which picture they mean (he no longer has access to any of his photos), but he thinks it was probably an intimate photo he captured of his son and wife together in bed one morning. ("If only we slept with pajamas on, this all could have been avoided.")

They say all of Mark's data has been deleted, forever.

The idea that we would tell tech companies to "permanently delete accounts suspected of trafficking in child pornography" is a seductive one. But these companies aren't courts, they don't have anything like a due process system—and yet, they can dole out penalties that go beyond anything that a court would impose. Even if a judge sends you to prison, the state won't incinerate all your family photos, all your correspondence and every personal file you have. It won't cut you off from every other account you have.

Google made a mistake. So do judges. When judges make mistakes, you have the theoretical possibility of appealing. When Google makes a mistake, you don't even get that theoretical chance.

If we are to punish people who traffic in child sex abuse materials (and I think we should), those punishments should be meted out by a publicly accountable justice system after a fair trial that adheres to the bedrock principles of due process. It shouldn't be meted out by unaccountable corporate giants who get to punish you in ways that far exceed any court's reach.

13

What about Warranties?

We've all seen a sticker that reads "Warranty Void if Removed," usually covering a screw-head or access panel. Maybe that sounds reasonable to you: if you go messing around inside the guts of your gadget or your car or your appliances, how can you expect the corporation that made it to honor its warranty?

Congress took up that question in 1975, and it came up with a much more nuanced answer. The Magnuson–Moss Warranty Act *requires* companies to fix their stuff if it's defective, even if someone else tried to fix it first (companies can only force you to use their official service depots if they'll fix it "within a reasonable time and without charge"). They can't void your warranty just because you used someone else's accessories or replacement parts—HP can't void your warranty for using third-party ink or third-party paper.

Those are the rules, and they've been the rules for nearly half a century. They were the rules through the entire consumer computing revolution. They were the rules through the whole internet era. If those rules were unduly onerous—that is, if it were impossible to run a tech company without control of third-party service and modifications—then none of those gadgets, devices, services and tools that have defined the past forty years of digital tech would exist.

The rules on warranties predate the consumer tech revolution. Every would-be tech mogul knows or should know about those rules. If they're too emotionally fragile to run a business where third-party repairs and add-ons exist, they should choose another career. That's their problem, not ours.

14

What about Poor Countries?

In the roil over Poland's 1505 constitution, the Polish Parliament adopted an act called *Nihil novi nisi commune consensu*: "Nothing new without the common consent." The nobles in parliament declared that the King could no longer make consequential changes to the laws of their land without the nobles' consent.

In the 600-plus years since, *Nihil novi nisi commune consensu* has given way to a catchier slogan: "Nothing about us without us." The modern term began in the disability rights community, where it meant that decisions about how to accommodate disabilities should involve people with disabilities. The slogan was also taken up by Indigenous activists, who used it in opposition to a half-millennium's worth of paternalistic—and genocidal—policies that treated First Nations people as children at best and livestock at worst.

Nothing about us without us is a pretty good principle for any group of people. You know that saying, "So easy my mom can use it?" I know, *ugh*. But it's actually worse than that: moms have rarely been in the room when new products are designed—not even products that are targeted at moms!

In 1969, Neiman Marcus's Christmas catalog featured a $10,000 Honeywell "Kitchen Computer," based on the Honeywell 316 minicomputer. The (all male) designers had been charged with creating a flashy, high-end, futuristic device targeted at mothers, and so they asked themselves, "If I were a mother, what would I use a computer for?" They enumerated all the ways that people used computers in 1969—insurers tabulating large data sets, payroll departments running checks, inventory systems running on large databases—and tried to think of parallels in the lives of imaginary mothers.

Eventually, they hit on a use-case: mothers kept boxes or loose-leaf books full of recipes, right? Well, a recipe was just a data structure. The Honeywell 316 could store a *lot* of recipes! The Kitchen Computer was born.

They didn't sell a single one (possibly because retrieving recipes required a two-week course in learning how to toggle binary switches on the computer's faceplate).

Most tech isn't designed for moms. Moms have to muster enormous reservoirs of patience, ingenuity and persistence to use most technology. If your mom is using a technology, chances are that doesn't mean it's *easy*.

Compare that to, say, *your boss*. When a technology doesn't work for your boss, they get to call up the IT departments and bark, "I don't want to hear any excuses, just make it work!" Your mom doesn't get to call up a tech company and do that.

We should really all be saying, "So easy your *boss* can use it."

Moms aren't typically represented on tech product design teams, but they're not the only group that's missing from those teams.

Western tech design teams are typically composed of well-off people with fancy degrees from excellent technical universities. There are a smattering of people from the Global South who win scholarships to those schools, get work visas, land jobs at tech giants and find their way onto product design teams, but they are a minority of a minority.

Technology design choices are made in high-income nations with stable governments, at least the pretense of the rule of law, and reliable electricity and internet access, and then they're shipped to the Global South where those design decisions utterly fail. Hardware repairs require unlock codes from authorized technicians who are thousands of kilometers away. Mission-critical programs require multi-gigabyte updates that must be separately downloaded to each computer over a metered, expensive, achingly slow network connection—and if the power or the network fails mid-download, there's no way to start from where you left off. Social networks expose information that feels innocuous, but exposes users to sectarian violence or harassment.

The list goes on and on.

Even where governments in the Global South pass laws to force companies to adapt their technologies to local norms and needs, these laws are hard to enforce. Tech giants may not have any assets, data or personnel inside a small, poor country's borders, leaving the state with few enforcement levers to compel a recalcitrant offshore giant. One of the reasons national firewalls have proliferated is that it gives some leverage to otherwise over-matched states: "Comply," they can say, "or we will block you at the border."

That's not much of a threat for a lot of firms, and it exacts a high price from people within the affected country.

But interop—especially comcom—represents an entirely new policy tool for both states and users in the Global South. States that choose to immunize their technologists from liability for reverse engineering and modifying technology tools can both incubate a domestic tech sector *and* adapt technology to local purposes.

Take GBWhatsApp: it's a free/open-alternative client for WhatsApp, the wildly popular messaging service that Facebook bought for $16 billion in 2014. GBWhatsApp was created by an anonymous developer in Syria at the height of the country's civil war, and since then it has spread around the world. In West Africa, GBWhatsApp is more popular than Facebook Messenger. It has a ton of features that adapt it to local circumstances, most notably support for multiple SIMs on a single device, which allows users to host multiple WhatsApp accounts on their personal phone. It also has important privacy features, like the ability to turn off the read-receipt messages that let the people who've messaged you know whether you've read their texts.

In Indonesia, gig-work drivers form cooperatives and associations that commission *tuyul* apps—these are apps that modify how gig dispatch tools work. Some are trivial—like an app that increases the size and contrast of the on-screen text so that older drivers can read it. Some do real heavy lifting, like the *tuyul* app that allows drivers to spoof their GPS coordinates in order to trick the dispatch service into thinking that they are standing by adjacent to a station when a big commuter train pulls in. The dispatch algorithm won't assign a ride to a driver unless they're right next to the station, but this is an incredibly dangerous traffic jam to be stuck in, so drivers wait around the corner and rely on their *tuyul*-spoofed GPS data to get them jobs, which they zip in and fulfill. It's safer and more efficient, but it's much harder to convince a distant offshore algorithm designer to fix this oversight than it is to simply fix it yourself with a *tuyul* mod.

That, after all, is the most durable advantage that domestic technologists have over their rivals working for giant tech companies in rich countries: they understand the local context in ways that no one in a Silicon Valley boardroom can possibly match.

Today, poor countries in the Global South have generally terrible tech policies, driven by the US Trade Representative and US industry lobbyists. For example, I once guest-taught a master's program in international relations at a European university that attracted government officials from all over the Global South.

After my lecture on DRM, the former national librarian of a Central American country took me aside and told me that when her country was negotiating a free trade deal with the United States and the head negotiator called her and urgently asked, "What is anti-circumvention?" and she answered, "Don't give them anti-circumvention!" He replied, "They say we can't sell them our soybeans unless we do." They did—their anti-circumvention laws are even worse than the US version.

Then there were the negotiating sessions for the World Intellectual Property Organizations' Broadcast Treaty, which would have created new, even further-reaching anti-circumvention obligations on all UN member states. One day, in the hallways outside the main room, I was approached by the delegate for a sub-Saharan country that had UN "least-developed nation" status.

He wanted to know why I was so opposed to the terms of the Broadcast Treaty, given that I was there representing an American NGO and America had already passed laws that covered everything in the Broadcast Treaty and more. I told him it wasn't true and showed him that some of the treaty's provisions would actually be *illegal* in the United States. He got a very grave look and muttered something about going to find Mr. So-and-So.

I asked a colleague who this Mr. So-and-So was, and my colleague said: "That's the rep from the American National Association of Broadcasters. They've been traveling around the region, stumping in all the national capitals to get them to back the Broadcast Treaty." "Stumping," in this case, meant "lying."

As I write this, the South African Parliament is debating whether to adopt a new copyright law. It's hugely controversial, thanks to aggressive lobbying by US industry associations; they object to a proposal to incorporate US-style "fair use" into South African copyright, which would enshrine the same rights for information users as they enjoy in America. These corporate associations argue that while wealthy Americans should have flexibilities such as the right to make copies for educational purposes, poor Africans should not.

The Global South labors under a dual imposition: they are coerced into passing tech laws that are friendly to US corporations, and then those same corporations make unilateral product design decisions that do not account for local circumstances and, thanks to those laws, can't be modified by their Global South users.

Poor nations in the Global South are unlikely to be able to effectively administer interoperability mandates for Big Tech firms; these firms will simply withdraw their assets and personnel from the borders of any country that attempts this.

But these same countries can protect their domestic technologists who engage in comcom to directly modify those products to make them fit for purpose. In so doing, they can nurture a domestic tech sector and attract other technologists from neighboring countries who have great ideas that can't be realized at home.

15

What about Blockchain?

It's an established fact that 99.83 percent of all conversations about blockchain are nonconsensual. I wrote this section before the spectacular implosion of the crypto market, and as we go to press, the crypto collapse continues apace. It may well be that by the time you read this, it's more of a postmortem of a defunct fad than a critique of a current mania, but on the off-chance that someone out there is still trying to get you to trade your perfectly cromulent money for their magic beans, I'm going to leave it in.

I wasn't always a blockchain skeptic, but today, I am a confirmed "no-coiner"—that is, someone who has no time or interest in blockchain-based technologies. I arrived at that position after literally hundreds of hours' worth of conversations with blockchain advocates and after reading dozens of "white papers" and other materials that purported to explain how blockchain could check or reverse the worst excesses of Big Tech.

I found them entirely unconvincing. The problems that blockchain technologies say they will fix are inevitably not the problems that I'm worried about.

For example, there are various proposals for blockchain-based social media, with posts, or identities, or both, hosted on immutable ledgers.

I'm skeptical of these overall. These ledgers' immutability is inextricably bound to a speculative market in some kind of token that incentivizes third parties to either "stake" or "mine" crypto assets. The speculative value of these assets is tied to a volatile and entirely mutable belief that they will continue to appreciate, and if that belief collapses, it takes the tokens with it, and the immutable ledger ceases to be a reliable source of ground truth.

But let's stipulate that these ledgers are stable, that the environmental problems of proof-of-work can be shed by transitioning to proof-of-stake, that proof-of-stake's intrinsic oligarchic nature (proof-of-stake is predicated on the idea that the richest people have the most power to determine how the system works) doesn't produce any second-order harms to the system's trustworthiness or reliability, and so on—does this fix social media?

Not at all. The hard problems of reforming social media are the laws that block interoperability and the management of tech giants' unwillingness to provide interoperability in the absence of these laws. Because Big Tech can lock people into its silos, it can impose high switching costs on users who have the temerity to leave those silos: they can make you surrender your apps, or your data, or your relationships, or your media, or your customer list.

None of that is solved by creating a blockchain service, not even with all the above stipulations, because the mere fact that your alternative to a Big Tech silo runs on the blockchain won't make the giant whose customers you're hoping to lure away from a Big Tech service make their departure easy. The problem with Big Tech silos is that they're silos, not that these silos have the wrong database architecture.

Here's an easy formula:

if: problem + blockchain = problem − blockchain
then: blockchain = 0

Adding blockchain to something that *isn't* Big Tech doesn't change the Big Tech problem you're trying to solve *in any way*, so blockchain can't be adding anything to the solution.

I could write an entire (tedious) book about why I think blockchain-based technologies are foolish at best and scams at worst, but it wouldn't convince anyone in blockchainland of anything. In my discussions with blockchain people, I've encountered a persistent pattern: first, they assume that if you disagree with them, it must be because you don't understand them. If you manage to convince a blockchainist that you *do* understand them and that you *still* disagree with them, they assume you're being *paid* to disagree with them.

The only other group I've observed this pattern in is Scientologists.

Given that I'm not going to change anyone's mind here (if you're a blockchain person, you're probably either already sending me a long email accusing me of failing to understand blockchain or being paid to oppose it), I'm tempted to end this section here, but I want to raise one more important point about blockchain technology as it relates to artists' rights: the royalty schemes built into some pitches for NFTs.

In case you're reading this in the near future when NFTs are largely forgotten, let me refresh your memory. NFT stands for "non-fungible token." It's an entry in a blockchain—that is, a public ledger designed to be visible to all and alterable by none—that consists of four parts:

- a URL for a file somewhere on the internet
- an identifier for a seller
- an identifier for a buyer
- a computer program called a "Smart Contract" (optional)

For example, an NFT might read, "A user called Fred123 transferred https://www.whitehouse.gov/wp-content/uploads/2021/01/white_house_grounds.jpg to a user called Wilma456." The strong implication here is that Fred123 *owned* https://www.whitehouse.gov/wp-content/uploads/2021/01/white_house_grounds.jpg and sold it to Wilma456.

If you load up https://www.whitehouse.gov/wp-content/uploads/2021/01/white_house_grounds.jpg in your browser, you'll see a picture of the White House grounds. It is in the public domain, because it is a work of government authorship, and in the USA, all such works are presumptively not copyrightable. (This is a good policy! If the public funds the production of a work, the public should be able to freely use that work.)

But though Fred123 doesn't—and can't—claim any copyright to that image, he can still publish an indelible record on the blockchain that implies that the image is his and that he is transferring it to Wilma456 for some quantity of virtual "money."

Additionally, Fred123 can attach a smart contract to this NFT. A smart contract is a combined financial prospectus and computer program.

Like a financial prospectus, a smart contract specifies who owes what to whom and under what circumstance. This is written in finance jargon, and requires a high degree of sophistication to parse.

But the other half of the smart contract is a computer program, one that converts the text of the prospectus into a series of software instructions. This program is written in a computer language like C#, SQL, Solidity, Rust or JavaScript. This, too, requires specialized skills to parse.

If Fred123 or Wilma456 want to assure themselves that the smart contract they're executing actually reflects the deal they believe they are striking, they will have to ensure that both the prospectus and the program are faithful to that deal and written without bugs or loopholes that could subvert it.

The skills needed to understand a prospectus are pretty rare; likewise the skills needed to parse a software program. But the Venn diagram overlap of people who can read a software program *and* a prospectus is more like a *sphincter*.

Practically speaking, both parties to this smart contract are going to have to trust an outside expert to validate one or both parts of it. There are lots of opportunities for mischief here, especially since, by design, smart contracts execute themselves *automatically* and *irrevocably*. That means that if someone does figure out a loophole and exploits it, that exploit will happen without the possibility of a human referee overseeing the transaction and stopping it before it runs, and without the possibility of a financial institution or regulator ordering such a transaction to be reversed.

It is possible to construct a smart contract that only executes once a third party—called an "oracle"—has been consulted and has signed off on it. This adds both expense and risk to the smart contract: expense, because the oracle doesn't work for free, and risk, because the oracle may make a bad judgment call, or be hacked by a bad actor who can sign off on all kinds of bogus transactions that, once again, can't be reversed.

Likewise, some smart contracts are designed to be updated after the fact in order to eliminate bugs that are discovered after the contract is signed; this also creates enormous risk, because the third party who has the power to rewrite smart contracts could abuse that power, or lose control over their keys to an attacker who uses them to abuse that power—and, once again, if that attack is successful, it cannot be reversed.

So far, these are all problems common to every smart contract: very few people are qualified to understand them, and if you fail to identify a bug in advance it is usually impossible to fix it, or to reverse its consequences. If you throw in an oracle or two to prevent this, you lose virtually all of the putative benefits of smart contracts (that they are automatic, neutral, etc.), add expense, and friction, and then introduce a host of impossible-to-resolve trust issues on top of all that.

But let's assume that both the buyer and the seller are versed in esoteric finance jargon and esoteric programming languages. Let's assume the seller isn't claiming ownership over a work they didn't create or don't have the rights to. Let's assume that both the prospectus and the program in the smart contract are flawless.

We're still not out of the water.

A major selling point touted by NFT boosters is that the smart contract can embody a perpetual royalty arrangement whereby the originator of the underlying work is paid a share of every resale, so if I sell you an NFT of a story I wrote, and include in the smart contract the right to sell it or license out film adaptations, I can also include a clause in both the program and the prospectus where every time you resell my story or sublicense a new adaptation, 10 percent of the purchase price for those transactions goes straight to me, automatically, through the smart contract.

Here's how that program would look, in pseudo-code:

```
if [(resale) or (sublicense)]
then
send ($TOTAL_AMOUNT * 0.1) to #DOCTOROW_WALLET
endif
```

In other words: if the smart contract encounters an event called a "resale" or "sublicense," it will send 10 percent of the total amount to my wallet.

Now, say you want to do a sublicense deal, but you don't want to pay me my 10 percent. You could do a deal on an exchange where they call a "sublicense" a "sublicense_1." When the transaction is processed through the smart contract, it will check to see whether it has any subroutines pertaining to an event called a "sublicense_1," and, finding none, will simply ignore the event, and I won't get my 10 percent.

Bear in mind that if the prospectus prohibits you from doing that, and if the prospectus is a legally valid contract, then I can sue you, because we have a contract.

But we could do that irrespective of whether we had a smart contract. The ability to sue someone for breach of contract isn't a feature of blockchain technology! It's a feature of contract law.

Remember:

if: problem + blockchain = problem − blockchain
then: blockchain = 0

When I explain the problems of Big Tech to blockchain aficionados and they insist that their blockchain technology will fix things and then explain *how* they think it will do this, it never makes any sense. It's as if my house were on fire and they kept on insisting that they'd developed a *really good* burglar alarm.

Further Reading, Listening and Viewing

This book crystallizes two decades' worth of advocacy, writing about and working on issues of digital human rights. In writing it, I relied on several million words' worth of blog posts, archived at both boingboing.net/author/cory_doctorow_1 and pluralistic.net.

I have attended hundreds of conference talks and presentations on the subjects of this book, and a few stand out as significant:

- Yochai Benkler: After Selfishness—Wikipedia 1, Hobbes 0 at Half Time (Berkman Klein Center)
- Sumana Harihareswara: What Would Open Source Look Like if It Were Healthy? (Github)
- How Markets Co-opted Free Software's Most Powerful Weapon (Benjamin Mako Hill, LibrePlanet)

There are far more podcasts worth your time than you can possibly listen to, but there are some that anyone interested in tech criticism really should tune in to, including *Trashfuture*, *Tech Will Not Save Us* and *This Machine Kills*.

On tech and competition, I recommend the blog *Naked Capitalism* and Matt Stoller's newsletter *Big*.

You might think that law review articles aren't your cup of tea, and in the main, you're probably right. However, I strongly implore you to try these three open-access, highly accessible, recent landmark papers. The first is Lina Khan's "Amazon's Antitrust Paradox," published in 2017 in the *Yale Law Journal* when

Khan was a third-year law student. Today she is chair of the FTC and is turning the ferociously argued material in that paper into national policy. Second is Dina Srinivasan's 2019 Berkeley Law paper "The Antitrust Case Against Facebook: A Monopolist's Journey Towards Pervasive Surveillance in Spite of Consumers' Preference for Privacy," which makes a hugely important connection between privacy invasions and antitrust harms. Finally, there's Kate Klonick's 2018 "The New Governors," from the Harvard Law Review, which is essential to understanding the speech implications of monopoly platforms. Of course, there are a lot of books you could read, besides this one, if you want to learn more about the subjects covered herein.

On monopoly:
This is a golden age of anti-monopoly books, but even amid all that plenty, three titles stand out. The first is Zephyr Teachout's *Break 'Em Up: Recovering Our Freedom From Big Ag, Big Tech, and Big Money*. Teachout is a campaigning law prof who writes like a muckraking journalist in this accessible, infuriating work. Next is David Dayen's *Monopolized: Life in the Age of Corporate Power*. Dayen is a prominent journalist with a keen appreciation of the law, and his book is full of beautifully explained case studies. Finally, there's Tim Wu's *The Curse of Bigness: Antitrust in the New Gilded Age*. Wu is another campaigning law prof—he was Teachout's running mate in a bid for the New York governorship—who coined the term "net neutrality" and served as Biden's White House tech antitrust czar from 2020–2022. *Curse* is a brilliantly argued, swift-moving critical history of the rise and fall of US antitrust enforcement.

For tech criticism:
Start with my Electronic Frontier Foundation and Verso colleague Jillian C. York's *Silicon Values: The Future of Free Speech Under Surveillance Capitalism*, the best work on content moderation and speech in a global context, hands down. For an older international perspective on tech and its impact on movements for self-determination, read Rebecca MacKinnon's now-classic *Consent of the Networked: The Worldwide Struggle for Internet*

Freedom. For a scathing, take-no-prisoners takedown of the ad-tech industry, read Tim Hwang's *Subprime Attention Crisis: Advertising and the Time Bomb at the Heart of the Internet*. For an equally ruthless insider's takedown of startup culture, read Wendy Liu's *Abolish Silicon Valley: How to Liberate Technology From Capitalism*.

On innovation:

Andrew "Bunnie" Huang's *The Hardware Hacker: Adventures in Making and Breaking Hardware* (2017) is half practical advice for would-be reverse engineers, half deep philosophy of how all new things are made by nonconsensually tearing down and rebuilding the stuff around you. Claire L. Evans's brilliant *Broad Band: The Untold Story of the Women Who Made the Internet* is a novelistic history of the role of women in the rise of digital computers, and comprises dozens of case studies about how neglected minorities produce innovation by seizing the means of computation and reworking tools to make them fit for purpose. Aaron Perzanowski's *The Right to Repair: Reclaiming the Things We Own* is a timely and urgent look at how tech monopolies use the rhetoric of innovation to punish actual innovators who divert their products from landfills, all in the name of increasing shareholder returns. Finally, there's Half Letter Press's long-overdue reissue of *Prisoners' Inventions*, a 2003 classic that collected the beautiful schematic drawings and closely observed technical notes of an inmate in California named Angelo, who documented his fellow prisoners' incredibly creative and inspiring works.

Finally, a novel:

Tamara Shopsin's *LaserWriter II*, a fictionalized memoir of Shopsin's time as a repair technician at TekServe, New York City's legendary independent Mac repair shop. Shopsin weaves a beautiful tale that is a hymn to community-scale technological self-determination. She is also a daughter of Kenny Shopsin, co-founder of Shopsin's, the greatest diner on Earth, where the menu has hundreds of options and parties of five may not be seated.

Index